How I Rob Banks

How I Rob Banks

(and other such places)

FC A.K.A. FREAKYCLOWN

WILEY

I dedicate this book to my wife, Jess. I would not be here without you; thank you for everything. Nothing I write here can express how much I love you.

About the Author

FC is an author, keynote speaker, co-founder of Cygenta, and former head of offensive cyber research at Raytheon. As an ethical hacker for the last three decades, FC has helped thousands of banks, governments, and other organizations advance their security.

He has shared his expertise in mainstream media, including the BBC and ITV, as well as popular industry podcasts such as Darknet Diaries (EP66). He has also been featured in printed media around the world, educating people about cybersecurity from a hacker's perspective.

His time as the head of offensive research at Raytheon enables him to bring to bear his knowledge of how nation-states and the intelligence community work with cyber weapons and how to defend against them. The decades he has spent legally breaking into organizations, both physically and digitally, have taken him around the globe in the fight against cybercrime.

As co-founders of Cygenta, FC and his wife, Dr. Jessica Barker, empower clients all around the world to understand cyber risk and the relationship between the digital, physical, and human elements of security.

An avid reader and polymath, FC enjoys trying new hobbies such as woodworking, pottery, and homespun science experiments—all while lacking musical talent, despite his best efforts.

Born in Colchester, England, FC now lives in the United States with his wife Jess and their cat Bubble.

You can find him at `www.cygenta.co.uk` and `@_freakyclown_` on Twitter.

Acknowledgments

This book would not exist without the dedicated work of the team at Wiley.

Krysta Winsheimer, without your commitment, I would still be on Chapter 1. My thanks to Pete Gaughan for your patience, Archana Pragash for your outstanding layouts, Melissa Burlock for the cover design, and—last but not least—Jim Minatel, who was optimistic enough to believe we could do this so quickly. And to the countless others who worked long hours to make this book: I thank you all.

Thank you to everyone who ever supported me in my journey.

I also want to thank those who did not support me, did not believe in me, or held me back—you gave me the drive to push on and do the things you didn't think I could.

Contents

Foreword   xv
Introduction   xvii

Chapter 1:   What Is Social Engineering?   1

Chapter 2:   330 Cameras   4

Chapter 3:   Expensive Doesn't Mean Secure   7

Chapter 4:   The Trolley Problem   12

Chapter 5:   High (Street) Security   17

Chapter 6:   The Psychology of Stairs   19

Chapter 7:   The Broken Arm Ruse   21

Chapter 8:   Crown Jewels Are Not Always Shiny   24

Chapter 9:   This Is My Office Now   27

Chapter 10: How to Use a Pen to Hack Any Door   31

Chapter 11: My First Kidnapping 34

Chapter 12: I Needed a New Computer 40

Chapter 13: Building My Own Office 43

Chapter 14: Letter of Authority 47

Chapter 15: Astute Manager 49

Chapter 16: I Can't Fly a Helicopter 51

Chapter 17: Doppelgangers Exist 54

Chapter 18: Stealing the Keychain 56

Chapter 19: It's Dangerous to Go Alone. Take This! 59

Chapter 20: The Gold Bar 63

Chapter 21: Plush Carpets 68

Chapter 22: Clean(er) Access 71

Chapter 23: What We Do in the Shadows 73

Chapter 24: What Do I Know about Diamonds? 77

Chapter 25: How to Crack a Safe 80

Chapter 26: Find a Safe Space 88

Chapter 27: Well, That Was Unexpected 92

Chapter 28: Opening a Door on Security 95

Chapter 29: How to Tailgate an Opaque Door 98

Chapter 30: The Guard Who Was Too Polite 100

Chapter 31: The Swan Effect 102

Chapter 32: What's in the Box? 105

Chapter 33: How to Bypass an Elevator Security System 107

Chapter 34: The Loading Bay 109

Chapter 35: The Escort 111

Chapter 36: The Staircase 114

Chapter 37: How to Bypass PIR Detectors 116

Chapter 38: ATMs 121

Chapter 39: Open Windows 124

Chapter 40: Security on a String Budget 127

Chapter 41: How to Bypass Padlocks 131

Chapter 42: Padlocked Gates 134

Chapter 43: The Security of Glass 138

Chapter 44: Trading Places 142

Chapter 45: How to Bypass Keypads 145

Chapter 46: E-Waste 148

Chapter 47: Fourteen Desktop PCs 151

Chapter 48: Spy Gadgets 155

Chapter 49: How to Steal Fingerprints 158

Chapter 50: Five Banks a Week 162

Chapter 51: Finding Out Too Much 165

Chapter 52: Needle in a Haystack 168

Chapter 53: Stealing a Purse and Keys 172

Chapter 54: How to Pick Locks 174

Chapter 55: The Porn Cupboard 179

Chapter 56: The Apartment Across the Way 182

Chapter 57: Magazine Shoot 186

Chapter 58: Double Trouble 189

Chapter 59: Fake ID 191

Chapter 60: Impersonation 195

Chapter 61: How Maglocks Work 199

Chapter 62: Personal Escort 202

Chapter 63: My Favorite Door 205

Chapter 64: Microwave Fences 208

Chapter 65: Discarded Passes 211

Chapter 66: Bypassing Speed Lanes 214

Chapter 67: The Case of the Angry Man 217

Chapter 68: Let's Play Doctors 220

Chapter 69: That's for Me! 225

Chapter 70: How to Use a Snickers Bar 231

Chapter 71: Taking the Bus to Work 233

Foreword

It is a common complaint in cyber security that we don't relate our complex and important subject to ordinary life in an accessible way. There is no such problem with *How I Rob Banks and Other Such Places*, which is what makes its publication so welcome.

For some years now, FC has been at the fore in highlighting the multiple dimensions of cyber security and showing how a complicated and chaotic tapestry of vulnerabilities can be exploited. He is a living, breathing advertisement for ethical hacking and protected research. He thinks like a bad guy but acts (and writes) as a good guy. In that way, he exposes us to the worst tendencies of human life—malevolent intent on the aggressor's part; carelessness and complacency from the defenders—and points us toward achievable, practical ways of reducing harm.

I spent nearly seven years setting up and then running the UK's National Cyber Security Centre, part of the intelligence agency GCHQ, from the end of 2013 to the middle of 2020. This was an important period in cyber security, with the evolution of nation-state threats and the explosion of organized cyber criminality (particularly ransomware). But as things changed, patterns emerged in the way attacks were being carried out that caused us to think again. One of the most important areas of change was to banish the nonsensical phrase "people are the weakest link" and focus instead on how real people with real jobs working on real networks can manage the online mayhem FC charts so magnificently so that they can get on with their work and their lives.

I only wish this often comical but always crucial compendium of cyber capers and capabilities had been available at the time, and I commend it to you now.

Ciaran Martin

University of Oxford

Founding head of the UK National Cyber Security Centre
(2013–2020)

Introduction

I'm standing in central London, it's 2:00 a.m., and I'm dressed head to toe in dark clothes. I also have on a balaclava, but it's rolled up into a small beanie hat. My arms are crossed tightly in front of me, and I'm lost in thought, staring at a large red stone building. Inside this fortress-looking building is a multinational trading bank. Someone behind me clears their throat and calmly asks, "What are you doing?" Without even thinking, let alone looking around, I answer with the truth: "I'm trying to work out how to break into this bank." The intake of breath behind me snaps me out of my thought process.

I then turn to the voice and see two policemen staring at me in disbelief.

But my job isn't just about breaking into buildings; it's also about convincing people to believe me, whether I'm speaking the truth or lies. So, I did what anyone would do: I talked my way out of that situation with the truth, by explaining what my job is.

The truth is always better than lies. If you're going to tell a lie, it should be simple, short-term, and preferably preplanned. Anything else can quickly unravel.

I have a very interesting job: I break into things. Not just buildings but also digital fortresses and anything and everything that has a security control.

I never knew what I wanted to do when I was a kid at school. All I knew was how to survive the extreme poverty and abusive home I grew up in and how to circumvent systems and processes to keep myself fed and as safe as possible. It was in these formative years that I developed the skills to get me into a career I never would have dreamed existed: legally robbing banks.

I have probably robbed more banks than any single person on earth. It's an odd job, but it is something I am really good at. My goal is often very simple: infiltrate the company, find the target, and see if I can steal it, whether it's a bar of gold worth over a quarter of a million pounds or an box files of documents. One thing they never show in movies is how damn easy it can be.

I started my career working for multiple security companies, having been at the forefront of social engineering and the physical intrusion industry as we know it today. I was then lucky enough to be the head of cyber research for Raytheon, a giant in the defense industry, where I worked hand-in-hand with multiple government agencies around the world. My role there ensured the continued safety and security of the five-eyes nations and their allies, and I will always be proud of the work we achieved. While there, I began to germinate thoughts of creating a cyber security firm like no other. Soon after, I started Cygenta alongside my wife, Dr. Jessica Barker, covering physical, digital, and human cyber security concerns. Our cyber security consultancy works with some amazing heavyweight clients around the globe.

In my heart and soul, I will always be a hacker, whether that is digitally or physically, as the thrill of gaining access to something is one that will never go away for me.

I have been legally breaking into places both digitally and physically for almost three decades. This book contains some of the most interesting, funny, and downright unbelievable things that have happened during my career so far.

In this book, you are going to learn a lot about banks and how they work. Not just banks but also government buildings, commercial offices, and much more. Interspersed throughout, I will show you some of the tools and techniques I have used to gain access to some of the world's most secure buildings. If you are looking to get into a role like mine, looking to defend against people like me, or are just a curious bystander, you will find something of interest in this book. I ask that you do not use anything you learn here for malicious purposes.

So how is any of this legal? Why have I not been locked up for robbing thousands of banks and stealing data and assets worth hundreds of millions? Well, clients come to us and ask us to break into their companies and then tell them how we did it; this allows them to shore up their security defenses before the bad guys come along. Nothing we do would be legal without a lot of paperwork and ensuring that we stick to the rules of engagement. I will cover more about this later in the book, but suffice to say that in all my years in this career, I have never broken the law or broken into something when I did not first have permission to do so.

In the writing of this book, I want to entertain you and show you a little of my world; however, first and foremost, I have a duty of care to not only our clients but also the companies, countries, and individuals represented in this book. So, for the sake of security, I have had to change minor details so as to not step over the line and reveal serious security flaws, some of which have never been fixed.

A lot of the work we do is not as exciting as one might expect from reading this book. It may surprise you to know that often there is nothing interesting about stealing something from a secure building; however, sometimes a small event happens that is either a helpful learning experience and/or hilarious. As I wish to share all the funny and ridiculous things that have happened during my work, I have integrated some of these tiny details into the larger stories for narrative reasons, for times when I cannot reveal a sensitive detail, or when it was just too good not to share but did not take more than a sentence. But I assure you that every single anecdote is real and as detailed and accurate as I can make it without breaking an ethical or contractual bond. Where possible, I have included photos that I took during assessments, and I have provided drawings to help illustrate techniques or maps for context.

Oh, and in case you are wondering what happened with the police and that bank I mentioned, I was able to explain my job, and after some convincing, they let me get on with my job. I broke in and "stole" millions of dollars!

I hope you enjoy this book as much as I enjoyed spending my career so far performing the feats to fill it.

FC aka Freakyclown

Chapter 1

What Is Social Engineering?

*S*ocial engineering is the manipulation of people and situations to gain access or information that otherwise is not available to you. Social engineering can sometimes be used to bypass physical security—mechanisms in place to prevent access by unauthorized people—but not always.

Organizations pay me to test their security. I use a combination of social engineering and physical attacks to do so. The security I test might be the locks on their doors, the security guards and receptionists, or their computer networks. Most often, it's all of those and much more, as you'll discover as you read about how I break into banks.

In my role as a security professional, I use psychology, body language, charm, flirtation, lock picks, and other tools to break in. Before all that comes a lot of preparation and paperwork.

Social engineering has a long history, albeit usually by another name—*scams*. Before we hear about my adventures, let's look at the first social engineering attack.

The best-known historical piece of social engineering is the Trojan Horse. While almost certainly a myth, it's mentioned in book 2 of the Aeneid, a book of Greek poems, and again in *The Odyssey* by Homer. As I am sure you know, the Greeks pretended to abandon the siege of Troy and left behind a giant wooden horse. The Trojans, thinking it was a gift from the gods, brought it inside their walled city. That night, the Greek warriors hidden inside the horse climbed out, killed the guards, and let the remaining Greek army inside.

1

I am sure you can see the moral of the story is about trusting what you don't know and letting them past your defenses. Computer viruses are often called *Trojans* because they are disguised as something benign. The myth shows the many things social engineering relies on: deception, a false sense of security, distraction, and making the target feel like they have succeeded—all the while playing into the attacker's hands.

Many years ago, I was asked to provide my security expertise to a prison in England that was prone to riots and escapes. My role was the opposite of most: they wanted me to prevent people from getting out rather than people getting in. While working in and around the prison, I was told the story of an escapee who used a method similar to the Trojan horse.

The prisoner noticed that two of the laundry machines were broken and due to be replaced. They had been disconnected, checked over, and left in a loading area. The day the removal team arrived to pick up the machines, he hid inside one, much as the Greek soldiers hid in the horse. Several miles down the road, he broke out of the machine and out of the lorry and escaped. (He was eventually recaptured.) I wonder if he had ever read *The Odyssey*?

Criminals use social engineering to perform all sorts of attacks, from what we call *phishing* email attacks to get passwords to huge fraud attacks that steal hundreds of millions of pounds.

While many criminals use social engineering to scam people, some people use it daily, sometimes unwittingly. Sales personnel, for example, try to convince you to do something you don't always want to do: spend money. Marketing is all about social engineering: time-pressure sales, discounts, and added values that don't really matter. Supermarkets spend millions on the placement of items in stores to get you to buy things. Why do you think there are sweets near the payment tills? Because you will be standing there in a queue, and your child will beg you to buy the sweets they just have to have. It's an easy sale.

Every day in your office, you make small, political movements, coercing someone to do something for you. I bet you didn't know you were a social engineer! Who doesn't know that smiling or flattery works to get your way? Consider how many times over the last year you got your way, and think about how you did it.

For my role to be effective, I need to manipulate people into performing actions they would not normally perform. This can be tricky. But my role also includes having skills that attack or bypass physical systems. You can be the best social engineer in the world, but you can't out-smile or flatter a fingerprint reader. A locked door will remain locked unless someone unlocks it, no matter how much you yell at it or ask it nicely to open. This book will show you some techniques and how they have worked for me over the last three decades of my career.

Social engineering is just a fraction of the skills required to do what I do, but it is an essential foundational ability. It will continue to be the number-one attack used by criminals, as it has been for thousands of years. Understanding why it works and how it's used is the only way to recognize how to defend against it and prevent yourself from becoming a victim. As you move through this book, enjoying the anecdotes of my funniest and weirdest moments, try to pick out the "red flags" you could have spotted to prevent each attack. This book is an educational tool as well as an entertaining read; absorb the defense lessons, and honor them by putting them to use in your life.

Chapter 2
330 Cameras

Understanding the environment that you are trying to protect is vital. Without an extensive understanding of how security will fit in the environment, you risk making it ineffective or, worse, making it work against you.

I was once tasked with breaking into a government building. This building was not in the UK, but unfortunately, I was! Therefore, I was unable to do any recon work myself before the actual break-in. However, there was a ray of hope: a work colleague had been at that site a few weeks earlier. Despite them having no physical security experience, I felt I could offer some guidance about what to look for, and they could report back to me so I could plan accordingly.

Here is the report I got back from them:

1. There are loads of doors, too many to count, maybe 20 or so with no guards. They all look open to me.
2. I don't think I saw any cameras. Maybe a couple—I don't really remember.
3. There was a security guard near the main entrance, but it's pretty open. You can walk in and get a badge and go in through the barriers.
4. It looks pretty open; I could wander anywhere I needed.

You can probably already guess that everything in this report was wrong. Once I turned up in the UK, I took a quick look myself, and wow—the building was a fortress.

There were many doors, but all of them were emergency exits with no way of being opened from the outside. I found out later that there were 330 cameras around and in the building. The main entrance was guarded by two security guards armed with guns at all times. No one was allowed into the building who was not expected; only those who were expected could approach the reception area and get a badge.

Obviously, my friend had been expected and so was given a badge; they weren't watched by security and barely wandered around the building. They also missed the roaming armed police presence in the building, the numerous cameras, and the man-trap systems to prevent people from moving from one part of the building to another, along with numerous other security features I shall not mention for obvious reasons.

So I was stuck with a seemingly impenetrable fortress of a building with more cameras, more armed police, and more overall security than I had ever faced.

I did what any professional in my situation would do: I panicked, called my account manager, and said I wouldn't do it.

I rarely suffer from what is known as *imposter syndrome*, the belief that I am not as good as others assume I am. But I felt as though I had been hoodwinked, which put me on the back foot and lowered my expectations about the amount of planning I had to do.

My account manager was brilliant; he told me to stop being stupid, that he had never known me to fail, and that I should get on with it. So I did.

I spent the next 48 hours watching, timing, planning, plotting, making notes, and consulting online resources. By the third day, I had what I felt was the only possible plan to infiltrate this incredible challenge.

Many hours later, I sat with my client, discussing how I had managed to get in and perform the tasks I had been assigned. We were in the security room, facing a bank of monitors and large screens. Several of the security team were busy spooling back and forth over my tracks: I had managed to evade most of the cameras inside easily enough, the tapes showed an odd glimpse of me but nothing that had been flagged as suspicious.

What was suspicious only in playback was my sudden presence in the building. I had appeared near the loading dock and was let in via a staff door by a friendly passerby. But how I got to that door remained a mystery.

As they scrolled through cameras, I helped pinpoint the moment I got in. In the very corner of a screen, if you paused for a few frames, you could see part of a shoe.

I explained that I had studied the building, layouts, and camera angles, and one had caught my eye. The loading bay was underground and had wonderful architecture, with a long ramp aligned very nicely with the sun at a specific time of the morning. The low angle of the sun and the camera position meant that for a few minutes during the morning, the sun entirely blinded one camera. All I had to do was walk down the ramp, slip past the camera in those few minutes, and hope that the security team could not see me.

I felt pretty smart. But I can tell you, they did not see it that way and thought I had somehow "cheated."

I mentioned that had I not been a simulated attacker, I could have shone a high-power laser at the camera and taken it out entirely. That would have had lasting effects on the camera and probably been spotted by the security staff, but it was possible, at least.

Interestingly, after I got to the internal door, it was locked. I had to bang on the glass and convince a passerby I had left my pass inside—and they let me in. Again, security culture let them down, rather than the tech.

Once inside, after thanking the gentleman, I walked off to the left and around a corner. The first people I almost literally bumped into were two armed police officers. I did not speak the language, which is always worrying with guns in the picture, but I casually nodded and walked by. Never interact with people if you can avoid it!

Chapter 3

Expensive Doesn't Mean Secure

In the security industry, companies are often duped into buying expensive solutions to perceived problems. Usually the salespeople don't mean to sell snake oil, but often they don't listen to the client or understand their needs and weaknesses. If you take one thing from this book, please let it be that "expensive does not mean secure." I try to explain to our clients that they should, as Jessie J told us in her 2011 hit single, "forget about the price tag"!

This story is a splendid example of a security solution being installed without the client, consulting firm, or builders understanding their areas of expertise.

I was tasked with breaking into the head office of a particularly large and well-known bank. As mentioned, one of the most important things you can do with a client is talk to them and really listen to what they are after. This conversation ensures that the client is not spending more money on a job than they need to and that what they are asking for is actually what they need.

After a lengthy conversation with the bank, it became clear that the job was an extremely specific case and unlike most assignments we take on. The client asked me to enter the building through one specific door. This was unusual because the test was against the door system itself, not an attempt to gain access to the building or information.

It turned out that a security firm had recently suggested an upgrade to the client, and the client had done what they were told without any further consultation. They had spent upward of £60,000 on *one door*: the target door. It was state of the art at the time of the job, meaning it utilized a lot of new technology that we take for granted now, such as remote camera modules, wireless access cards, fingerprint override, sensors to detect multiple people, and anti-pushing technology. Evidently, after all the time, disruption, and money involved in installing the door, the client caught on that they had been duped and decided not to use the same security firm to test it.

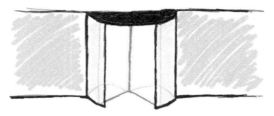

As with all security, it is important not only to understand the security device but also to understand it in the context of where it is placed. With that in mind, I must share the details of how this insanely expensive door was placed within the HQ of this wealthy bank.

The building had three entrances. The first was sometimes staffed by security and had a turnstile system (I will cover this later). That would be an effortless way into the building. The second entrance was temporarily blocked off and unusable because of broken glass that made it potentially dangerous. The third was where my task lay: the sophisticated £60,000 revolving door that the client had a lot of faith in.

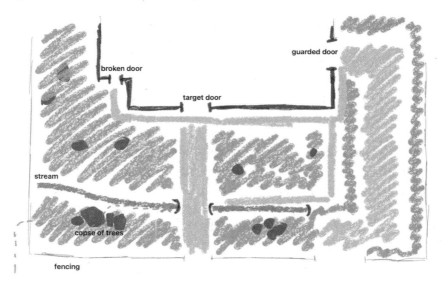

We start every physical security job with reconnaissance. The more reconnaissance you can do, the higher the success rate of the job. It can vary from hours to days of surveillance and intelligence gathering before attempting access.

I needed to spend some time watching the new door system to see if I could find a flaw that I might be able to use. The remoteness of the door made it impossible to get close and circumvent it physically; it also meant it would be hard, if not impossible, to attempt to clone the access cards being used. So, in the middle of winter, I pulled together my surveillance kit and headed out of my warm hotel room into the frosty night at around 1:00 a.m. I chose this specific night because it was moonless and overcast—both are important for sneaking around secure places at night.

I arrived near the site and hiked the last half mile to ensure that the car was not seen near the entrance. I was wearing my night kit: a selection of very dark blue clothes, including a matching balaclava. (Wearing black almost always makes you stand out more than dark blue. There is something uncanny about the color black, and humans pick it out subconsciously.)

I approached the fence line from one side, away from the main entrance, and noted the lack of CCTV cameras. The movie *Fight Club* portrayed a few things accurately: one was that a small piece of carpet is fantastic for climbing over a barbed-wire fence. I threw my small rug over the top of the fence and swiftly climbed into the compound. After removing the rug and tucking it against a nearby tree for later escape, I silently and swiftly made my way along the copse of trees and down to a runoff stream. I lowered myself into the stream and crawled along to get as close as possible to the door system.

Once I settled on the perfect spot, it was about 2:00 a.m. I was covered head to toe in cold, wet mud, and the water from the stream had gotten into my boots and soaked my feet. I knew I was in for a night of extreme discomfort.

I spent the next few hours in that cold, wet, muddy ditch peering at the door system through my night-vision goggles. It was covered by infrared security cameras, it had no keypad for a number code to override it, and security guards patrolled every 40 or 50 minutes, depending on how long they stopped for smoke breaks. Around 5:00 a.m., it started to snow—not fluffy Hollywood-style snow, but English snow, more akin to a Slushy being tipped on your head than the comforting flakes from *It's a Wonderful Life*. Life was not wonderful in that ditch.

However, my job is not to provide my client with minute-by-minute details of the weather and wetness of their ditches; it is to provide security advice. During those five torturous hours, I found a security flaw and formulated a plan. Around 7:00 a.m., before it got light, I hustled back along the stream to my rug-assisted exfiltration point and then back into the hotel. Once there, I took a quick, extremely hot shower, ate, and had a power nap before getting dressed in a nice suit and heading back to the site. It was time to see if my plan was going to work.

I'll attempt to give the narrative of what was captured on the CCTV. At 8:59, I am seen entering the path that leads to the door. As I walk toward the door, observant people would have picked up that my pace was deliberate. I glance at my watch and pause mid-step for barely a second. At precisely 9:00 a.m., I step into the door without interacting with the pass system. The door automatically revolves, and I stroll into the building.

As we reviewed this footage, the security team and the client looked at me and then back at the screen. They replayed it several times to confirm what they had just witnessed. The head of security, baffled at what he had now watched five times, turned to me and said, "Are you a Jedi?"

I explained to them the flaw I found. When a sophisticated moving door is installed, it is done not by security-trained staff but by builders. Like most of us, they work based on their experience rather than by following the manual. But such a door has a series of security steps that your average revolving door at a supermarket does not. Once the door is installed, the builders sign off, and someone else has to look after it and maintain it. But before the sign-off, the door must be tested. Doors like this have an "engineering" mode for precisely this type of testing: every 15 minutes, the door automatically rotates 180 degrees to ensure that the bearings are working, nothing is catching, etc.

During my five-hour vigil in the ditch, I noticed that the £60,000 door had been left in engineering mode. Every 15 minutes on the dot, it performed a rotation. I knew that if I timed it right and made sure I was inside the door entrance when it did this, I would have my way in. Even though I was observed by CCTV, security never caught me. CCTV is (almost) always a method of retrospective security to prove something happened and not an active monitoring system.

Reconnaissance pays off, and preparation is key. The actual test only took a few minutes, but the wet, muddy, miserable hours of observation led to my success.

Chapter 4

The Trolley Problem

Now and then, a job comes along that is so full of warning signs that you don't want to even consider taking it on. This one was one of those jobs. I should have been concerned that it was a government facility; that meant top-notch security. I should have seen the red flags when I was told the site was so sensitive that it had its own permanent police presence in a building next to my target. Still, I took the job and never regretted it.

For obvious reasons, I cannot give you much detail about the site. There will be no maps or geolocation specifics. But I *can* tell you that gaining access to the site and making my way across the grounds was one of the easiest jobs I had done to that point.

The site in this anecdote was like several other ultra-secure sites I have broken into during my career: they focus on stopping you from getting out rather than getting in—a very odd but specific security tactic. While most sites we deal with are built to prevent non-authorized individuals from gaining access, at a certain level, that often flips around. Ultra-secure sites tend not to highlight their security. For instance, consider this photograph my wife and I took on a visit to Area 51, the ultra-secret black site in the USA.

Note the lack of fencing, cameras, and other security measures you would expect at such a place. Another site with a similar approach is Fort Knox, the gold repository in Kentucky, USA (but they also have a standing platoon of soldiers and tanks to help shore up security).

While gaining access to this specific site was easy, accessing the building was the main point of this assessment. The client hoped I would never be able to gain access to the building, let alone sensitive files; but on the off chance that I did, I would have to prove that I could exfiltrate sensitive information.

After making double-sure I had found the correct building (I did not want to accidentally break into the police station), I utilized one of the methods described later in the book. (Sorry, I can't tell you which one because it worked.)

Almost every secure building has a mentality built on centuries of defense, from ancient castles to even further back: to set up a secure perimeter and only let in the right people. The technology has changed, but the mentality has not. Once inside the building, I had free rein to go wherever I needed, as is often the case.

While I was wandering around, chatting with people, and finding my bearings, I walked down a corridor with plastic skirting boards and dull beige paint peeling off in flakes. The lack of people in the hall, the poor upkeep, and the décor were subtle indications that management never came down here. This was the maintenance and logistics area.

The end of the corridor had a set of double doors that wouldn't have looked out of place in a restaurant, given the way they swung back and forth and had little round windows breaking up the government-beige paint. Behind these swinging double doors was a small, open room.

As I pushed into the room, I expected at least one or two people to greet me. However, the room was empty except for trollies and trollies of red folders. Red! I knew immediately that I had hit the jackpot. In the government world, classified material is often kept for years and is frequently stored in plain folders in big storage facilities. But when a satellite site like this one is working on transient data or information that has been shared with them from another agency, it is often stored in red folders. This aids in identifying classified materials that are to be destroyed when their use has ended. These red folders should be collected and put into a furnace. However, some sites cannot do this, so the classified data is loaded into a secure truck and transported to a specialist facility where to be burned.

The room I stumbled upon was a holding room. Either that site had suddenly finished using thousands of folders, or a collection hadn't been made for weeks.

I understood the sensitivity of the data in those folders. Given what the site was used for, I had extra knowledge of what was probably inside each folder. I did what anyone else would have done in that situation: I stole a whole trolley load. I didn't really steal it in the illegal sense—I had permission to take anything I wanted—but I was making a loud statement to the client.

I rolled the trolley down the corridor and into what could be described as part storage hall and part loading facility for lorries. I got the trolley down a small but incredibly steep slope that was clearly an afterthought in the design process for the dock and managed to open the loading bay door from the inside. Surprisingly, no one seemed to notice, care, or even observe what I was doing.

I decided to see how far I could take the trolley on its little excursion from its life of going back and forth in trucks. I rolled the classified materials past the offices, past the makeshift police station, and toward the main entrance of the site. I got as far as the public visitors' site before I realized that I had maybe gone a little too far and was in danger of putting myself and the data at risk. I quickly took the following photograph and, with the utmost care and speed, dragged the trolley back across the carpark, past two police officers who didn't seem to care about my trolley dash, and toward the loading bay, where the door was shut!

I had to think about what to do next: call for help (not great) or leave the data there while I broke back into the office and tried to open the loading bay door (not safe). What would you do?

Thankfully, I didn't have to do either. After a brief scout around with the trolley in tow, I found another way to gain access to the loading bay door and took the documents back inside without leaving them alone.

To this day, I don't believe anyone has removed as many physical classified materials from a secure location—and hopefully, they never will.

Chapter 5

High (Street) Security

With a lot of security, it is less about technology and more about the culture of an organization and the education of people.

The very nature of human beings is what often helps me to do my job. I'm lucky that my wife is a world-leading expert and author on the matter of the human side of security: this understanding is key to creating a secure environment.

No other story I have displays this better than the following anecdote.

I was tasked with gaining access to a small business. Nothing fancy; this particular site was one of many. However, unlike all the rest, this small business had maybe fewer than 10 staff, and the contents of the building were unbelievably important.

The importance and sanctity of the contents of that one tiny brick building, nestled in the heart of London, would astonish you. Hiding in plain sight, down a sweeping road near some high-profile offices, you could walk past this site a thousand times and never notice anything odd. Maybe you would eventually notice that the lower ground windows were not actually windows but bricked-up, painted façades to give the appearance of a normal townhouse.

In much the same way that some London houses are entirely fake to hide the tunnel outlets of the London Underground (55% of which is above ground), this site was a façade to an impenetrable box. The building, as I mentioned, was made of brick. The height of the roof stood above the neighboring buildings enough to prevent easy access, and the fire escape doors were secure enough to prevent opening from the outside. This left just one entrance point: the oversized black door with a large central gold knob and security device attached to the undercover vestibule.

Now, in a situation like this, I can do all sorts of fancy tricks. An infrared camera works well, as it picks up the latent heat from the keypad just after someone uses it. The downside is that you have to be quick and close. It also helps if you haven't loaned your IR camera to a friend the previous week and not had a chance to pick it up again; lesson learned! I could use special tape and lift fingerprints off all the keys and then only need to brute-force the order. I could even just bust it open and try to bypass the device itself; or maybe, as a last resort, I could use the pen trick (you'll hear more about that later).

I decided that I was going to have to try to get close enough to see the make and model; maybe it might give me a clue as to the best way to attack it. That's when Sarah happened.

Sarah worked in the building. Obviously, I have changed her name to protect her. While she is unlikely to ever read this book, I want to save her the embarrassment of what happened next.

It was around lunchtime, often the best time to attack any building, as the comings and goings of multiple people create a multitude of opportunities that can be exploited if you are ready and gutsy.

I observed people coming and going from the office over the course of half an hour. I noticed one woman as she left the building, shutting the door and trundling down the stairs and into the street, half reading her phone, half ignoring the homeless person she almost stepped on. Just then, another woman walked up the steps to the door. After standing for a moment, she turned and shouted at the first woman, who was now about 20 feet from her. "Hey Sarah, what's the code again?"

Rather than walk back 20 feet, Sarah did the unthinkable. In her gruff smoker's voice, with surprising enunciation, Sarah shouted the five-digit pin code to her colleague. Myself, the homeless person, several bystanders, and the woman at the door now all knew the code. The code was based on the year the building was built.

Thank you, Sarah. I couldn't have done it without you.

Chapter 6
The Psychology of Stairs

As I wrote this book, I wanted to create something more than just a collection of anecdotes—something more than just a strange biography of one part of my life's work. So, throughout this book, I've placed chapters such as this to introduce the techniques that I use to perform my work. Just promise me that you won't use these for nefarious reasons.

The following is a technique I have used on almost every engagement. It involves a bit of psychology and some social constructs, so bear with me.

One thing that is often overlooked in this type of work is the importance of blending in as much as possible: what we call in the security industry "the grey man." So it is important that you dress the part of the location you are trying to infiltrate. One of the key factors of this is to wear a jacket over everything. Whether that is over a t-shirt or a dress shirt, most people in the types of places I test wear some sort of suit.

Another important factor is that most office buildings are multiple floors, and for some reason I will never fathom, more powerful people work further away from the entrance. As a co-CEO of my own company, I do not wish to waste more time than I need to; why others decide that they need to spend that time getting to their office is bizarre to me, especially as they always want to have the nearest parking space. Anyway, I digress. The point is, the more senior people work on the higher floors, and even if they do not deserve it, they are often given more respect than those on lower floors.

Have you ever noticed how, when going up stairs, you will be inclined to give way to the person coming down the stairs? It's like an automatic right of way for whoever is descending.

You can really take advantage of this weird psychological effect to get into entrances you probably shouldn't.

Let me give you an example of a situation where this can come in handy. One of the simplest ways into a building is to use tailgating, which is essentially following someone authorized through a door. There are many variations of this, as I will discuss later, but almost everyone reading this book has done the basic version of asking someone to hold a door open for you. In a situation where you are trying to tailgate into a restricted-access door off a stairwell, if you walk up the stairs and someone comes out, they will literally be looking down on you and may even ask who you are and what you are doing. If, however, you are coming down the stairs, even if they do not know you, they will instantly assume you have seniority and probably hold the door open on your request, even from some distance.

So, the first thing that I do when gaining access to any building is to reach the highest possible floor as quickly as possible. This way, all tests I carry out will be downward. This also has the advantage that you get to a target quicker, and you are always working your way toward the ground floor, making escape much easier.

Oh, the jacket thing I mentioned: it is highly effective in this situation because when I reach that high point, I ditch the jacket. It was just part of the ruse to get into the building. Now without it, I am using other psychological tricks. In these kinds of places, people (and men especially) don't often go to work in a suit and not wear a jacket. However, most people would remove that jacket and leave it on a chair. So, by not wearing a jacket, I am visually signaling to people I approach that I belong. I have obviously left my jacket on my chair. This also doubles as a great excuse: "Oh, I left my pass in my jacket upstairs."

Finally, it can be a brilliant way to convince people to let you into a building, especially at lunchtime and during the rain.

If someone came up to your building and it was raining, and they had no jacket on, and they said they left their pass in their jacket inside, you would be more inclined to let them in. It would be awkward if you didn't and then had a meeting with them later on, especially if they turned out to be more senior than you. It's the nature of human beings to trust and help those in need—particularly if we think it might come back around to us.

Chapter 7

The Broken Arm Ruse

There are countless ways to gain access to a building. The odds are always stacked against the defender, and there is always at least one way to successfully compromise the target. One of the oldest tricks in the book, when it comes to lifting or pickpocketing, is the good old-fashioned pretend broken arm. For those of you who do not know about this, the attacker crafts a fake plaster-cast arm sling, maybe even with a fake hand sticking out the end. The crafty criminal can pretend their arm is broken while their real arm/hand is free to move around under cover of the jacket they are wearing, which is often modified with a slit to allow outside access.

When close to the mark, the criminal (or social engineer) will create some diversion, and the real hand will slither out and steal the target item and back into the jacket before anyone notices.

I have never resorted to this technique, but I can see its use, maybe not to lift anything of value, but perhaps to convince someone to do something like hold a door open that they shouldn't.

I would like you to keep that in mind as we delve into the next small story of how I was able to gain access to an interesting office space of an insurance company.

The company approached us with the task of gaining access to sensitive files held on the third floor of the building. The design of the building was rather odd, or at least unusual.

The front entrance was at the base of a glass-fronted stairwell. The reception area was not on the ground floor but in the middle of the three floors. Looking through the glass, I could see that the reception floor was protected by a pass system. This meant that I had to not only gain access to the front entrance but also time the ascent of the stars to coincide with someone coming out, whom I couldn't see. Tricky! Luckily for me, I had a few tricks in mind as to how to approach this second stage, and performing the first part turned out to be easier than normal.

As I've mentioned before, lunchtimes are almost always the best time to gain access to a building. Insurance companies often employ call center staff: generally underpaid, under-trained, young, inexperienced office workers. To be frank, they rarely care about the company's security.

The trouble with the odd layout was that I realized it was going to be hard to predict when someone would head to the front door. There were four paces between the bottom of the stairs and the front door. For me to successfully tailgate behind someone exiting the building, I would have to be close enough to take advantage. However, I wouldn't know if they were just heading to the stairs or the exit until the last moment.

After a few days of reconnaissance efforts, I decided I should attempt the infiltration as planned. I walked along the badly spaced steppingstone path that was designed to appear professional but ended up looking like they just ordered too few slabs and spaced them out. I pretended to be reading something in depth on my phone as I approached the front door. What I was waiting for was to see someone exiting reception wearing an outdoor jacket; this would tell me they were leaving the building rather than heading to the front door. As planned, I saw two gentlemen walking down the stairs with jackets on; I jogged forward a little bit to meet them as they exited, and as predicted, they held the door open for me to enter, probably assuming I had just swiped my pass. I then went up the stairs, bypassing the ground floor, as that was not my target. I avoided the reception floor and headed up to the third level. It is incredible to me how many companies do not take into consideration the impact design can have on security. Here they had hidden the front line of defense, the reception area, behind doors that no one was forced to go through.

Having reached the last five or six steps before the door to the goal floor, I started to mildly panic that I might be forced to hang around, which could raise suspicion. But by the time I got to the third step, the security door opened.

Standing there, looking at me, finishing the last few steps, was a small man radiating the impression of milquetoast. His arm was in a plaster cast. The point, however, was that despite his struggle to push the heavy security door open with one arm, he was delighted to see someone. I leaped forward to offer some aid. I helped him leverage the door wide and held it open for him to exit.

In his eyes, I was a savior, someone who was able to help him escape the confines of his workplace for 45 minutes. But to me, he was the ultimate skeleton key, and he had no idea who he had just let into his office.

So, what appeared to be a challenging task at first turned out to be a literal walk in the park. And all thanks to a man with his arm in a plaster cast. Sometimes in my job, fate deals you a strange helping hand, and you just have to take it. Sometimes that hand is at the end of a plaster cast.

Chapter 8

Crown Jewels Are Not Always Shiny

It is not all gold bars and fancy equipment that I steal. A few times, we have worked with small companies. Like Cygenta, the company I run with my wife Jess, these small companies have few staff; maybe it's their first office, and they are taking security seriously.

On two particular occasions that I can recall, the client had some odd ideas about what they felt constituted their most valuable asset. I find it funny that some peers in security will often be heard saying, "Protect your crown jewels." We all know what they mean by that, and I have no doubt said it in the past, too. But we need to qualify what we really mean. Some companies will just assume it the asset with the biggest price tag, maybe it is a gold bar in their safe (that story later), or maybe it is the new helicopter (also later). But what I mean by "crown jewels" is that piece of data, that thing, that object or person, that if it were to be stolen, kidnapped, or destroyed, would render the entire company broken beyond recovery.

We often go through a set of questions with new clients to get an understanding of what they are trying to do and, more importantly, what the driver behind it is. Sometimes, though, you cannot stop someone from spending money on something they do not need but really want.

Two clients had different assets in mind for us to try to steal. The first was an exceptionally large TV, the sort that is mounted on the wall in a large boardroom—the kind of TV that even if you were to unbolt it without the three people in the same room noticing, it would take three people to lift the damn thing onto a cart to remove.

24

We spoke at length about the feasibility of what it would take to perform the operation; in the end, the client finally saw sense that the most important item in their office was not, in fact, the expensive yet quite easy-to-replace TV they had just bought but, in fact, the CEO himself. He was one of those serial-preneurs before the term was even coined. He had no interest in the company itself and was just going through the motions of making the company look bigger and more secure than its shared, rented building to increase the value of the company so he could sell it.

We ended up not performing any physical security testing on his office building but rather performing an open source intelligence (OSINT) assessment on the CEO. OSINT is the collection and aggregation of all resources that are publicly available: for example, Facebook, Twitter, LinkedIn, articles, interviews, and even website breaches. This proved more valuable to the board of directors than the original security assessment would have been.

The second client provided drawings and designs for small architectural companies. This client had a treasure trove of data that, if stolen, would be useable by criminals to undermine upcoming projects. But this data was not what the client felt was the most valuable asset to their company. To them, it was a gigantic plotter. Essentially, a plotter is a very large printer. Some, like this one, can print six or seven feet wide. They were determined that if one or more of these went missing, their company would end, because their main source of income would be removed—no printer, no prints! These are not exactly quick or cheap to replace, either.

Despite all my efforts, they went ahead and commissioned us to steal a plotter. A lot of jobs are difficult to execute because of the security of the building. Not so much this one. In this case, it was the size of the item.

It was trivial to gain access to the building via a window on the second floor, and it was just as trivial to bypass the passive infrared (PIR) system they had in place to set off the alarms. However, what was nearly impossible was the removal of the plotter without rendering the device inoperable and without any assistance.

Bear in mind that I was on the second floor of a building with no elevator, with an object on wheels that measured around eight feet long and a foot and a half wide. I was grateful for the wheels!

How do you steal an eight-foot, wheeled printing device down a staircase? Well, you can't, not easily, under those conditions. So, I did the next best thing. I rolled the plotter across the entire floor and out the fire exit straight onto the flat roof that covered the side of the building.

Now I admit, this was not really what a criminal would do, but I must work within the confines of certain limits that they do not. The client did not want their asset ruined in any way just because I needed to prove I could fit an eight-foot-long device down a circular fire stair! However, the photo I took of the plotter sitting in the middle of the roof during the night certainly caused the right reactions by the client. We were able to remove the plotter from its "secure" location, just maybe not to where they expected it to be.

Chapter 9

This Is My Office Now

Every now and then, a job goes so well that when you write up the report, it seems unbelievable. When this happens, it feels like luck and the universe want you to do something awesome—and they also want you to get home early.

I had a tricky task this time: a very secure building on a very secure site. What's more, the goal was not just to gain access to the building but to gain access to physical files (and more) that were held on the most secure floor. The files were accessible to only four people and kept in a secure enclave at the end of an exceptionally long corridor so no one could accidentally walk down it. The office was staffed 24/7: at a minimum, there was one staff member in there, and often there were two.

In this story, I'm not going to share the details of how I managed to gain access to the site. Similar methods are described in this book, and I have a duty of care to clients to not give away all their secrets. Let me just tell you that I got in.

After gaining access to a secure site, it is polite to contact your client, explain that you are there, and keep them informed of your progress. After all, then they may not intervene if they hear about a security alert; this way, they are aware of the situation.

I decided to meet the client in the staff canteen, a low-slung building with glass-fronted doors and a blackboard menu that touted the soup de jour. It was about five past nine in the morning; I was not in need of soup, but I had cracked step one on this test.

The client and I agreed to continue the test, and several minutes after I left him, I was texting him to let him know I was not just in the secure building and past all of the company's fancy protections but actually on the secure floor and heading down the corridor of doom toward the target files.

One thing you have to do in this job is be nice. I have heard that people like to shout or scream and throw around fake authority to get a person to do something for them, but for me, it's more effective to be nice. As the saying goes, "You will catch more flies with honey than with vinegar." This is true in all of life, not just social engineering.

I approached the secure lair of the four file keepers with trepidation. After all, I had no idea how they would react to a stranger entering, nor did I know how many would greet me.

It turns out my timing was impeccable. One person was just leaving and said "Hi" as I walked past them down the corridor. As I rounded the corner, I saw four doors: one shut, two ajar, and the other fully open. Only one person was at their desk. I introduced myself, and he (well, let's call him Neil) introduced himself. As we talked I started to mention about my made-up role and how it was my first week, and I was being given all the crap jobs. The job I was doing today was collecting and verifying asset tags, those annoying bar codes companies put on everything they buy to make sure items don't end up on eBay. It's a thankless task to crawl around on the floor under desks and write them all down.

Turned out the team didn't get any visitors, and in fact, their requests for help from IT often went unanswered for days. Boy, were they happy to see me—and even happier that I could help with some of their unanswered computer issues in return for Neil helping me.

After I had been there a while helping, the other staff member returned. We were introduced (let's call this person Doris), and I was promptly volunteered to help fix some of their issues. After about half an hour, I mentioned that it was time to get back to my work and that I needed to write up a bunch of notes before heading off. At this point, I had to trust in the friendship I had built in the last 30 minutes or so. I gathered my things and walked over to one of the empty offices where the door was ajar. I said over my shoulder, "Do you mind if I just sit in here and write up my notes?" and, not waiting for an answer, let myself in and sat at the desk. No one voiced any concerns. After a few minutes, I gently and very slowly started shutting the door until it was almost closed, hiding what my real intentions were. I pulled some of the files off the shelf and began taking photographs as proof. Like you see in the movies, when the spy breaks into the target's lair and starts taking pictures with a small camera—that was me, except it was a small camera phone.

After taking enough pictures, I felt it was time to update the client. I decided to use my new desk phone: after all, why not?

I leaned back in my seat and called the client. He asked where I was and whether I'd had any success. I told him where I was and what was going on, and he couldn't believe it. So I invited him to a meeting in my new workspace. I told him to come up to the secure floor, and I would show him just what I'd been up to.

A few minutes later, my mobile phone rang, and I answered it to find the client saying he couldn't come in. He was being blocked by the security system. He wasn't allowed on the floor at all. I guess it wouldn't be a secure floor if everyone was allowed to roam around, right?

So, I stuck my head out the door and asked Neil how to buzz someone in, as my boss was coming to check on my work. Neil replied that I needed to ask Dave about security. I walked out of the office and down the corridor and found the wandering security guard milling around the kitchen. I explained that I had an important visitor waiting at the door and he was to show him in; in exchange, I would finish making his coffee. He immediately ran down to the door and let my client in.

I spoke with my client as we walked into the long corridor. "I have never been on this floor before. I don't think many people have," he said as he gazed around, taking it all in. We got to the little enclave, and I walked him into my new office and shut the door behind us. He was now aghast at where we were. In fact, he was starting to get agitated that the files were open and on the desk, and

I realized that he was starting to show the signs of panic because he might get in trouble for being there.

I suggested that we head back to the canteen and get something to calm him down. As we left the office, I waved and said goodbye to Neil and Doris, and they waved and said cheerio to me. I said thanks to Dave for his help, and he thanked me for the coffee.

As we were leaving the building, the client, still in shock, turned to me and said, "I have worked here for nearly 10 years. In that time, I have never been onto that floor or met those people. You have never worked here, yet in two hours, you have not only been on that floor but also managed to get yourself an office in the most secure area, and everyone on the floor knows you by name, and apparently they love you. It's all too much to take in. You've been worth every penny, but no one will ever believe me!"

I'm sharing this story for two reasons. The first is to illustrate that being nice is usually more powerful than being nasty. And the second is to highlight that security issues can often be caused by factors outside of security's control, like company culture and whether people feel ignored or included.

Chapter 10

How to Use a Pen to Hack Any Door

This is a short recap of a test, not because nothing happened —several remarkably interesting things happened during the assessment—but because I can't talk about those incidents in public. It is the curse of someone who does this job. You often do a thousand mind-boggling things, but for security reasons, you can never talk about them.

What I *can* tell you about is a technique I often use to gain access to locked doors that are infrequently opened. Infrequently used doors are a bane to a social engineer and physical intrusion professional like me. To perform tailgating, you need to be able to reliably work out when and where a door will be opened. Frequently accessed doors are perfect for that type of attack. The converse are never-used doors; that type allows time to perform other attacks such as lock picking or bypassing the security system, maybe even destructively (if that's within scope) without fear of being seen or heard. But infrequently used doors are the worst. They aren't used often enough to tailgate, but they are used too often to pick, hack, or open with brute force.

What makes this type of door more difficult is that it often has a magnetic lock system rather than, say, a normal key lock.

This is where I can use my pen to bypass the locking system. It may seem that a pen cannot defeat a decent security system, but almost all security doors can be bypassed using this method.

The beauty of this technique is that you can try it at home or in your office to see how well it works. It does take a bit of practice, but

31

once you understand the mechanics, much like riding a bike, you will never forget.

The technique goes like this:

1. Find a large pen. It must be thicker than the gap at the bottom of the door. This is vital for the technique to work—it cannot pass under the door.
2. When the coast is clear, approach the door and lean the pen against it, resting one end against the crack between the door and door jamb and the other end on the ground, as shown here.

3. Walk a safe distance away and wait.

When someone opens the door, the pen will fall inward between the door and the door jamb. As the door swings back and tries to shut, the pen will block its path and keep the door ajar. This pen-width gap will prevent any locking mechanism from kicking in and leave the door unlocked.

It is highly unlikely that the person using the door will notice the pen. Occasionally, they see the pen and either ignore it or pick it up. Do not use an expensive pen you care about! A Mont Blanc pen will go missing, but a cheap gel pen in glitter green probably won't.

You have to be cautious about which way the door opens. Inward openers are preferable due to the way the pen falls. However, with some careful practice, you can get this technique to work on doors that open outward toward you. (Many times, when I first started using this technique, a pen would go flying across the car park when someone was a bit too vigorous as they left work.)

Be aware that sometimes door systems have backups that can put you in jeopardy of being found out. One such system, especially on infrequently used doors, is a "door-ajar" alarm that alerts security that someone or something has prevented the door from shutting completely and locking. But in my experience, such alarms have a time lag to prevent false positives—so be sure to leap at the unlocked door and retrieve your pen as soon as possible. I'll cover how to bypass maglocks a little later in this book, including how to prevent these types of alarms from going off while allowing you later access.

Chapter 11

My First Kidnapping

Everyone remembers the first time they kidnap someone: the rush of adrenaline, the fear of it going terribly wrong, the sense of urgency, and how wrong it feels.

I have been fortunate enough to do some insanely cool things in my extensive career. I have been flown around the world to interesting and beautiful places. Due to childhood trauma, I do not have the best memory for faces and names. However, I always remember a building if I have broken into it. In some cities, I can navigate just by using these landmarks in my head.

One such place will live in my mind forever because I was able to kidnap someone there. This is not something a non-criminal normally ever does. So, it's an understatement to say that it was a "can't buy this" experience.

I say this was my first kidnapping, but really I mean it was my first commercial one. (The rest were silly hazing rituals.) So I came to this with a bit of experience.

I had a client with a particular problem that needed to be checked. Like almost every bank in the world, they had lots of computers: not laptops or desktops like you may be used to, but large, powerful machines called *servers*. Such servers are the backbone of a bank through which every transaction travels—every stock trade and savings account, billions of dollars in 1s and 0s that make up the binary world I help keep secure.

Servers generate a lot of heat and use a lot of electricity. They need to communicate with each other as quickly as possible, and to top it off, they need to be redundant so nothing stops if something breaks. So, servers are best kept in special buildings called *data centers*. There are several types of data centers, and we will get to some of them later. But this client had a regular data center: massive, but still regular. A few staff worked at the data center, and due to the high value of the data it held, it had a high proportion of security staff.

My job was to infiltrate the building in any manner. I had carte blanche to do anything, even break things. As long as I did not injure or kill anyone, the approach was up to me. The budget was healthy, and the contracts were solid. There was one drawback: the main reason for the test was that the bank had hired a third-party security team made up of ex-Gurkha guards. These fearsome warriors were highly trained military professionals. The saving grace for me was that, being based in the UK, they were not allowed to have guns or the impressive traditional kukri knives Gurkhas are famed for wielding.

So, in the middle of summer, this was how I found myself waiting and watching a building on the outskirts of an industrial estate. I staked out the place in a silver Ford Focus rental car, watching the main gate day and night to find and record events and possible ways in.

After several nights, I thought the security staff had started to get suspicious of me; I saw them watching me watching them. So, I had a wonderfully weird conversation with the car rental company, asking to replace the car with a similar-sized vehicle. I ended up with another silver Ford Focus—just what I didn't want—but that's all I could get. I hoped the security team assumed it was another car and not that I had swapped the plates.

By the end of the week, I had a solid plan. Well, a plan that in my head might work 50% of the time—as solid as it gets. A shift change happened every evening. I watched as members of team B arrived and parked their cars and team A pulled back from the gate and fences and congregated around the entrance to the building. Shortly after, teams A and B went into the building, leaving one member at the curb as a lookout.

I assumed that teams A and B were doing a handover, exchanging paraphernalia and keys, passes, etc., and probably doing some paperwork. All in all, that exchange took 10 or 15 minutes. Then team B members made their way to posts and began roving patrols, and team A members left in their cars.

Two interesting things to note before we move on. First, the gate was double-gated, which meant it could act like a trap. It was also double-wide. Its normal operation for a car arriving was like this:

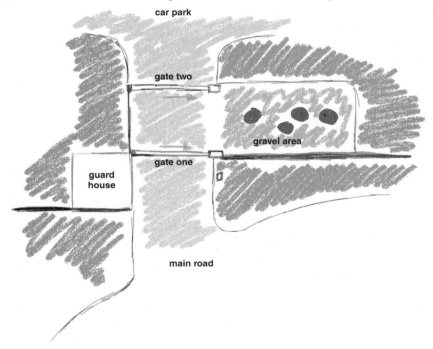

A car pulled up, and the driver either used a security badge to open the gate or spoke remotely to the person in the guard house, who checked for entry requirements and opened the first gate. The car pulled forward, and the gate shut behind it. The second gate then opened and let the car into the parking lot. The exit procedure was slightly different, and this is important. When a car pulled up at the inner gate, a sensor in the ground automatically opened the first gate and then began to open the outer gate before it started to shut the inner one. There was an opportunity for overlap: with a small enough car, perfect timing, and enough speed, you could theoretically wait for a car to leave and make it through both open gates.

The second thing to note is that although the same actions happened in the morning and evening, the evening routine coincided with regular staff members leaving.

So there I was one evening, waiting in the car with the engine running, my heart pounding in case my plan went horribly wrong. (Things often go horribly wrong very quickly, but experience and training always help in such situations.) I watched the team B members arrive one by one: 7 of them, which brought the total to 14 Gurkhas on site. Team A fell back and filed into the building, leaving the gate unguarded for the next 10 minutes.

The timer began. I had less than 8 minutes. After what felt like hours, a staff member walked out of the building. They went to their car and sat in it for what seemed like another eternity. Eventually, the staff car pulled up to the inner gate, which started to open. I made sure my safety belt was on tight and the engine revs were building. This needed to be flawless.

The second gate pulled back slowly, grinding its way fully open. The first gate began to shut.

The staff car pulled out and turned left, away from me. I floored it (well, as much as you can in a Ford Focus). The tiny tires squeaked as the car shot toward the gates.

At 30 mph, I careened through the first open gate, bracing for impact as I almost clipped the wing mirror on the second gate post. Now doing about 40 mph in a parking lot designed for 5 mph, I relaxed for a moment that lasted as long as it took to realize I needed to pull off the second part of my plan. The scarier part.

I kept the accelerator planted as I veered the car not onto the twisting roadway to the entrance but straight through a small designer hedge. I bounced over the larger-than-expected curb and decimated the little hedge in a shower of sparks, noise, and branches. That was more fun than it should have been.

You may be surprised that the airbags did not deploy. This was because I had anticipated a collision at the gate and removed the Restraints Control Module 7.5 amp fuse from the car—which was lucky, as I had not planned the off-road excursion.

I removed my seatbelt as I slammed on the brakes. The curb had taken a lot of the speed out of the car already, so I didn't need to slow too much to stop it. The lone guard was standing next to the car, caught entirely by surprise. He later told me that he thought the staff car had lost control and was worried I had injured myself.

What happened next I think shocked him more.

Within seconds, I had extracted myself from the car. Before he knew it, he was face down in the backseat footwell, his legs shoved in after him, and the car door shut. The poor fella was trapped upside down in a strange car. This was shock and awe in full action—the only way I could even begin to get ahead of a trained warrior security guard.

I had expected more of a fight, to be honest. But before he could begin to figure out what the hell had just happened, I was driving the wobbly wheeled, hard-to-steer Ford back toward the main gate. By my calculations, I had about 3 minutes before all his mates piled out, caught up with us, and gave me a good kicking.

I came to a halt just down the road and explained to the chap exactly who I was and what I was doing. I showed him proof, and, to my surprise, he completely understood the situation. I breathed a sigh of relief, and we both chuckled as the adrenaline drained away. The security staff had been warned that a test might be coming, but they expected it to happen several months later.

I convinced him to go along with the scenario now that he had been incapacitated. He handed over his security passes, etc. He lay down in the back seat, choosing that option over standing in the street or getting in the trunk. I drove what was left of the Ford back to the gate a few minutes after team B took their posts and used the security pass to let myself in. I parked and told the Gurkha in the back seat to wait until I got back. With the keys to the kingdom, I infiltrated the building and gained enough further access to prove that I was able to get in.

Despite the damage to the hedge and the car, my first kidnapping was a resounding success!

Kidnapping Addendum

While my work often leaves a long-lasting impression on clients, it is not often that I do a follow-up after a reassessment check. But in this case, an interesting event happened about a year later. I was working for the same client, and as part of a digital penetration test, I had to go onsite to one of their data centers. It happened to be the same building.

I turned up, and as I went through the security procedures (properly this time), I caught the eye of a security guard. He came running at me. I was sure it was the guy I had bundled into the back of the car—was he going to attack me? I froze, unsure what to do, and then I saw that he had a huge grin on his face!

I have rarely been greeted with such enthusiasm; he was jumping up and down with excitement. He grabbed me and pulled me into the security room, screaming, "This is the guy, this is the guy that kidnapped me!" He was delighted to be able to share his story and introduce me to his colleagues, he even commented that they assumed he had wandered off from his post that day. As I said at the start, it's rare that a non-criminal kidnaps someone, but I must be the only one lauded by his captive, Stockholm syndrome aside.

Chapter 12

I Needed a New Computer

This anecdote explains why it is vital that everyone in your company knows what you do and understands that if they ever see you, they should act as if they do not know you. In this case, I had been asked to break into a small secure building for a client. Unknown to me, the company I was working for was doing other work for that client, which happened to be going on at the same time I decided to perform my attack.

During this assessment, my colleague, let's call him Rod, was on site to witness the attack. As for his reaction to seeing me in action, well, I shall do my best to retell his side of the story for you later.

My target was a small room that contained a maximum of eight staff members. It was down a dog-legged corridor that offered no way to get a clear view of what was happening in the room. I had to go in blind and do, well, pretty much anything just to prove to the client that I had made it there.

I managed to gain access to the building rather easily by tailgating my way into the ground floor. Once in, I was able to locate a stairwell and shoot up the steps three at a time. Despite a few odd looks from people surprised to see someone with such enthusiasm climbing the stairs, no one really cared I was there.

As the building was pretty small, finding my way to the target dog-legged corridor was painless. I listened at the corner and could hear nothing, or at least no one seemed to be walking toward the corner. I did not have a plan for what I was going to do inside the room. Who knew how many people were in there, how they would react, or even if the door was locked? I had to adapt, think on my feet, and react quickly to any situation that arose.

I strolled down the corridor toward a cheap wooden door like you find in many offices and quickly peeked through the round window with its wire mesh "security" glass. I counted three people in there, eight desks, and—wait, there was a fourth person, hiding behind the monitor on the desk that faced the door. The tiny office was essentially packed: as it held a maximum of eight people, I was bound to be noticed. Due to the large monitor in front of them, I couldn't identify the fourth person, but I knew the other three worked there.

I had already been spotted by the people in the room, and often in these situations, it's better to move forward than try to retreat and cause more suspicion.

As I burst through the door like I owned the place, I quickly reconned the room for anything that could help me. Everyone watched me except the guy behind the monitor, who, despite his best efforts to hide, I now recognized as Rod, my colleague, there doing some other work.

Behind and to my left, on the floor between me and the desk, was a PC. It was unplugged and unused. Maybe it had just been replaced, or maybe it was going to be a replacement soon. The point was that it was not in use, not plugged in, and would not cause any disruption if I took it.

In a second, I accepted the plan that just popped into my head and bent down and scooped up the PC, said "Thanks" to no one in particular, and walked straight back out the door.

That's my side of what happened. In a debrief later, Rod was able to tell me his side of the story as it unfolded before his eyes:

"I was sitting in the office of the client when I noticed a face pop up and peer through the round window of the entrance. I realized it was you and almost immediately started laughing. I ducked behind the monitor so no one could see or hear me, and then suddenly, you burst through the door. I then saw you, without any hesitation, and like you were just not going to let anyone stop you, pick up a PC that had been placed there only about an hour before by IT. You picked it up and strode out with such confidence that as soon as the door shut, someone said, "Well, I guess IT changed their mind about that new PC,' and everyone went back to what they were doing. I just sat in fits of laughter, knowing exactly what had happened and how royally screwed they were all going to be in a short while."

What he meant was that either IT would discover the missing PC or the head of security (my client) would be telling everyone off in that building and especially that room—apart from Rod.

Chapter 13
Building My Own Office

W hen you have an office, people respect you. It can take years of grinding away in the corporate world to rise to the ranks where you are given an office. Sometimes in this job you have to take what you want; this is how I got my own office in an FTSE 100 company in just a few hours.

A client brought me in to test the security of their site: a site that was so large it had four distinct buildings, and each of those buildings was massive. The site had third-party security guards who roamed around like you see in the movies, always vigilant, and no one was sure if they were keeping people out or keeping people in. At least that was the image they portrayed and, no doubt, the image they projected in their sales pitch.

Once on the site, I was able to easily slip past the first reception area, and beyond that point security seemed to be rather lax. As in many of my assessments, I had agreed to perform multiple actions against the target. This is often due to time limits or if the client is feeling confident that I won't achieve the main goal. What normally happens is that I end up doing most, if not all, of the intended actions.

This job was one of those where I was easily able to accomplish all the tasks handed to me and still had hours of time paid for by the client. I like to give our clients as much value for money as possible, so I decided to continue finding my own things to do. In the end, it meant more writing for me, but I figured it might make a cool story one day. Oh, it has already!

While wandering around one of the four buildings, I stumbled across a curious location: a vast open area on the ground floor. It had two doors, one from the corridor and one into a blank partition wall. It was huge, 40 feet by 40 feet, and completely and utterly empty.

It didn't take long for me to decide that if I was going to stay here on site for the rest of the day, I needed a base; in fact, I needed an office.

I stood and thought for a moment. This could be a teaching lesson, and I was pretty sure I could pull it off.

I started a mental list of what people need in an office. A table, a chair, a PC, a phone—these seem the minimum for an office, right?

So, to challenge myself a little and to see if the security guards were any good, I decided to build my own office. But to make it harder, I had to steal all the items I needed from different buildings.

I started with the table. I wanted a big desk, but the practicality of one person moving a desk made me reconsider, so I went for a fancy glass one, instead. I found one in the building that had the space for my office—which was lucky, as it was heavy. It was holding a few plant pots and such, so I chose it because I knew it would be sturdy. I manhandled the glass desk into the office space and put it near the window.

The desk phone was easy to remove from one of the other buildings—child's play, as they say. I walked in and saw a bunch of hot desks, those temporary workspaces, like a timeshare for workers to sit at when they come into the office. I found one not in use. I ducked under the table, unplugged the phone, and swiftly walked back to my office.

I needed a PC: slightly harder to acquire because I had to find one not in use so as not to disrupt anyone's work. As I had spent a few hours performing other tasks, I had a few ideas in mind about where to get one. After about 15 minutes, I acquired a PC and then had to go back and get a monitor, too.

There remained one major item I needed so I could settle in and pretend to do some work: a chair. Where on earth would I get a fancy chair to sit in? Well, marketing has all the creative people, so I decided they would have the most comfortable chairs. I wandered into the building housing them and found an unused desk. Maybe the employee was on vacation. It didn't really matter; what mattered was that the chair was definitely not being used, and the employee was now donating their chair to the office of FC.

I wheeled the chair to the elevator and down to the ground floor. This is where I had my first real problem.

The front of the building was protected by five-foot-high glass barriers, the sort where you swipe your badge and they swoosh open like a *Star Trek* knock-off. You might be wondering how I got past them to get in; well, you're in luck, I wrote a whole chapter about how to bypass glass pedestrian barriers in this very book.

Anyway, a spot to the side of the barriers was double-wide, used for loading large items like a chair. I was trying to get it to open when I saw a small group of staff coming into the building.

"Oi mate, you won't have any luck with that barrier. You need to call security to open it," chimed one of the group to me across the lobby.

"Well, that seems a waste of time; I am just trying to get my chair outside," I dejectedly replied, throwing my arms around to animate the lost cause of my adventure of chair-napping.

You might expect, in this situation, that they would ask me why the hell someone would want, let alone need, to remove a chair to the outside of the building. But people don't question things as much as most of us expect, especially if you act like you know what you're doing. Instead, this kind group immediately felt sorry for me, or maybe they just didn't like dealing with the security people either. Led by Cheerful Charlie, they took it upon themselves to collectively "stick it to the man"—"the man," in this case, being the security guards who had so far failed to interact with me at any point.

Cheerful Charlie stood for a moment as the cogs in his head whirred and produced a plan. It was the plan I wanted him to suggest; I had been willing it along with wild, flaying arm animation akin to what a man would look like when fighting off bees, had one not been able to understand that he was throwing a chair into the air.

"What if we helped you pass the chair over the barrier?"

The next five minutes entailed the five of us trying to lift a swiveling office chair up and over the barrier, culminating in loud cheers and high fives when the chair was liberated into the sunshine of the day. I wheeled it across the garage to my soon-to-be-completed office space.

The photo shows the lovely office I built, taken by my client as proof of what I was able to accomplish.

One small detail that is not visible in the photograph that might make you smile, especially if you are the Cheerful Charlie, who helped me that day. See the wall behind me in the photo, the big partition wall with the other door? Behind that door is the main office of the third-party security guards. They had been coming in and going out and passing through my office the whole time I was building it, and never once did I get questioned about what I was doing.

Chapter 14
Letter of Authority

How do I do my job and not get arrested? The key factor is, of course, that I have permission. But it's easy to say that; how do I prove it? Imagine a scenario where you are trying to break into a bank and steal millions. Halfway through breaking in, security rolls up and starts screaming at you and trying to take you into custody. How do you prove that you are indeed there doing what you are doing under the remit of the very place you are trying to break into?

The letter of authority is the single most important document you can have when doing this type of assessment. So what is it?

Essentially, the letter of authority is the only proof I take on an assessment to prove that what I am doing is, in fact, an assessment—and not a crime.

The letter should include both your name and company as well as a very detailed explanation of what you are doing (known as the *scope*). This is then followed with detailed instructions as to what the security team at the company should do if you are "caught." The instructions often include contacting key C-suite persons at their listed emergency contact numbers.

My letters always say that the security team should use their internal communication methods to contact the staff listed and not use the numbers printed on the letter itself. You might find this odd, as their names and numbers are included right there on the letter. The reason is that I always make sure I have created a fake letter along with the two real letters I carry at all times.

The fake letter is another ruse and another part of the assessment. Listed on the fake letter are the correct names of internal contacts but the mobile numbers of my own colleagues who are on hand to potentially get a call during the test.

When called, my colleagues pretend to be the points of contact internally and instruct the security team to stand down. If this works, the client security team has failed that part of the assessment because they didn't follow the correct process. After all, a criminal could easily take a fake "letter of authority" with them while breaking into a building, with fake contact details to confirm their identity.

The two real letters are always on my person, and how I handle the letters is a reminder that small details can make a big difference. Never leave them in a hotel, and don't even put them in your jacket pocket, which might be discarded during the day. Keep track of where the fake and real letters are so that you don't get them mixed up. This is vital if you get caught.

During my long career doing this, I have thankfully never been caught. Only once have I had to show my letter when a job went wrong from the client side. I talk about that exciting moment in Chapter 69, "That's for Me!"

However, a colleague with whom I had shared this subterfuge letter method did have to use a letter once. I received a message from him that he was attempting to gain access to a secure warehouse and I needed to be on alert for pretending to be one of the contact people in his letter of authority. A few hours later, my friend was caught, and security read his fake letter and called me. Preparation saved my friend. I was able to pretend I was who they needed to think I was, and I told them to stand down, give full access to my friend, and even ensure that he was escorted to specific locations and allowed to leave with his target assets. Security can be a weakness if you know how to subvert it.

This is a great example of how the letter of authority can be very useful and yet, in the wrong hands, can be an automatic win for anyone trying to gain entry to a secure or valuable area. Security and staff must be aware of this kind of duping and that "verify, then trust" is a sensible approach but only works when you verify in the right way. Look at Chapter 15, "Astute Manager," for how this can work.

Chapter 15

Astute Manager

We have just spoken about the power of the letter of authority and how and why it is needed in my job. Sometimes that the letter is used outside of being caught. One of these times is at the end of the assessment if the client contact is not onsite.

I often call such meetings when I have completed my task. They generally involve me explaining my situation to the senior staff member. This happened once during a bank heist.

I had successfully accessed the bank and gained entry to its secure section. This was not your average high street bank, but rather the type that doesn't keep cash onsite.

I walked up to a staff member and asked them to call the manager. They were unsure how to respond at first but eventually complied, figuring the manager would know what to do with this stranger. A few minutes later, the manager appeared and ushered me into a small room. I explained who I was, where I was from, and what I had been doing. I could see the panic rising in the manager, and I wanted to nip things in the bud before they called the police. I handed over the real letter. There was no point kicking them when they were down; they had failed so massively in other areas that it didn't seem worthwhile. They had much bigger problems.

The manager left the room, clearly suspicious. Eventually, after what felt like far too long, they confirmed my story. They had taken things very seriously and had escalated through the correct chain of command to reach the correct point of contact via their internal system. The reason was that the manager was well trained: although their initial reaction was surprise, they quickly fell back on their training, and suspicion once again took over.

I was told that they had looked at my letter of authority and dis-covered it was a fake: a little surprising, because it wasn't—this was the real deal! I asked the manager why they thought it was fake. The devil is in the details. They had noticed that the letterhead wasn't the bank's current letterhead at that time.

These assessments take a long time to put together, to ensure that everything is done safely and within the law. This often leads to long delays between setup and performing the assessment, com-pounded by multiple C-suite executives being too busy to sign the same document. The letter I had with me was more than a month old, and since then, the branding team has updated the letterhead used by branches. Fortunately, this branding issue didn't impact the outcome of the assessment. Still, branding can be a significant issue, especially with time delays.

Chapter 16
I Can't Fly a Helicopter

My job is to help people make their businesses more secure, and my job involves doing a lot of very odd things that a lot of people will never get to do, from climbing down elevator shafts at a bank to kidnapping people. However, there is one assessment that sticks out in my mind above the others: the time I was asked if I could steal a helicopter.

That's right, a client asked me to steal their helicopter. I was unsure how to respond to this request; after all, it was a hospital, and it was a brand-new Airbus Eurocopter H145 they had purchased. I was unsure for several reasons. First, didn't I just mention it was a hospital? I don't like to disrupt any business continuity, let alone remove a vital lifesaving system.

Second, and probably even more pertinent, I have no idea how to fly a helicopter. I mean, it can't be that hard, right? But at that point in my life, I had never even been on a plane; I had a fear of flying. But I figured helicopters work in a similar fashion to planes—just in a more brute force beat-the-air-into-submission way than, say, gently gliding through the air. Taking off shouldn't be an issue; just go full Jeremy Clarkson, scream "POoooWEeeeeRrrrr!!!!" and throttle up until it moves. Landing might be trickier, but that's just controlled crashing: do it slowly enough, and any landing you walk away from is a good one, right? There would be the issue of the bill. They had just spent almost £16 million on the helicopter. I supposed that in small enough installments, I could maybe pay it off eventually.

Despite my reservations, I accepted the challenge. I had no expectation of getting near the thing, but who knows, it could be a fun job. Who could say no? In discussions with the client, we agreed that getting into the helicopter was going to be the goal and would be ample proof that I could have stolen it.

These types of assessments take a lot of planning—lots and lots of planning. Many times, I have been in a hotel room with building plans strewn around the room like some *Ocean's Eleven* scene, hoping that room service doesn't ignore the Do Not Disturb sign, find my heist notes, and call the police.

As with most physical jobs, there are rules and regulations to abide by. I have to obey the law, and I have to stay within the confines the client's need. The one piece of wiggle room I have is the date of the attack. While we try to make sure as few people know about it as possible, to make it more realistic, it's not always possible to keep this circle small, but it works better if we can. In most circumstances, although we don't pick a specific date, it's more a large range of days. This allows us the advantage of jumping on opportune moments or avoiding days when we see something that might make it harder, such as additional security on site for some reason.

It was very near the beginning of this date range when another client canceled some work, which left me free for this helicopter heist. The date range we gave was some months wide. But here I was, kitted up and ready to go in the first week. Recon had gone smoothly so far; then, just as lunch was nearing its end, an opportunity afforded itself to me, and I leaped at it.

About 25 minutes later, I found myself in the bowels of the hospital making my way through the tunnels that run under most hospitals and into the more private areas. This would allow me to come at the pilot area in a more unusual way.

I popped my head into the changing room and didn't see anything cool like you would expect: no helmets hanging on hangers, no jumpsuits. This wasn't going to be like that Clint Eastwood movie, *Firefox*, where he breaks into the Russian jet fighter by dressing up as a pilot and strolling out to the plane. Nope, I was going to have to go in jeans and a shirt and face whatever was up the stairs.

It was around the time I started up the steps to the helipad that a vital bit of information I was missing presented itself to me—one I had failed to even start to imagine I would need.

How do you get in a helicopter? Do you need keys?

I called a friend, and similar to the scene in the original *Matrix* where Trinity calls Tank and says, "I need to know how to fly a Bell 212 helicopter," I found myself saying, "Dude, how do you get into an Airbus H145?

Before he could google the answer, I swung the door open onto the roof, my legs heavy with lactic acid as I climbed another set of stairs onto the helipad.

"Never mind," I said, and hung up.

There was no helicopter. I was utterly disappointed and pretty relieved, all at once.

I never got to crash a helicopter or even sit in one. The client was pleased, as the test of security highlighted what they needed to fix. For them, the goal wasn't to steal the helicopter, of course, but to see if I could have. They later told me that there had been a massive delay in the delivery of the helicopter, and it was going to be delivered three months later than expected due to some shortage or other.

Since then, I have always secretly wanted to know if I could have flown it. Almost certainly not, but at least the client was very happy with the result, and they didn't have to replace a £16 million wreck.

A couple of years later, I not only got over my fear of flying enough to travel several times around the globe on planes but also got a chance to fly one (but I didn't steal it).

Chapter 17

Doppelgangers Exist

For those of you who do not keep up with myths and legends or have never played Dungeons & Dragons, there exists a creature that can impersonate another: a doppelganger. *Doppelganger* literally translates from its German origins as "double walker"—a ghostly apparition of another living being. In this case, mistaken identity played a key role in my ability to infiltrate a client's building.

Washup meetings or debriefs are vital to any assessment, whether a physical assessment or a digital penetration test (pentest), that gives a company an overview of its digital vulnerabilities before criminals find the same faults. Even if the assessments are successful—and particularly if they are not—debriefs allow the client and I to go over every step and learn from mistakes or issues. They allow us to have an honest dialogue about what happened, when, and how. Many people overlook them, but to me, they are one of the most important elements of a test.

A debrief of a particular physical assessment made me stop and pause and led to the client having a serious chat with the CEO.

I have already mentioned many times that a key aspect of physical assessments is dressing the part. I have also mentioned that my job is to find the lowest bar of security. This often means my dress code and behavior degrade over time to see what triggers a security reaction.

I had been going into this building over the course of a week. At first, I dressed smart/casual like the rest of the teams. But by dress-down Friday, I appeared in ripped jeans, a slogan t-shirt, and a baseball cap I am known for wearing at all times. I had free rein around the building; people held the door open for me without my asking, and I was able to move things around, sit in offices, and generally act like I owned the place. It was strange.

Surely there was an obvious explanation for this behavior. I brought it up in the debrief, and the client was at a loss; he couldn't understand it, either. It should be noted that my client was new in his role; this assessment had been set up and arranged by his predecessor, and he was as new to the company as I was. In fact, I had been in the office more times than he had.

He went and spoke to the heads of several departments and returned with a photo frame—a tad odd, but stranger things have happened, especially in this line of work.

The photo he handed me was from the CEO's desk. It was a family photo taken at a sunny resort in South America.

It turned out the CEO had a son who was a similar age, similar height, and (unfortunately for that kid), similar appearance as me. There I was—no, there *he* was—standing in South America in a baseball cap.

The CEO's son, my doppelganger, had an annoying habit of walking into the office like he ran the place; and everyone just let him, because he was the CEO's son. They all assumed that I was him and let me do anything I wanted, dress how I wanted, and cause havoc, all while being deadly afraid to say anything to anyone, least of all me.

It was the most bizarre outcome of any assessment I had ever done. The CEO was informed, and the son was immediately banned from entering the site. The CEO took it well and started a training and outreach system for the departments to change the behaviors and reign of terror the employees were experiencing.

While we were not able to help at that time, one of the core things we do at Cygenta is change the culture of a company. My wife, Dr. Jessica Barker, is an award-winning global expert in security culture. She leaves me in awe with her knowledge of things I could never start to understand. Here's what she says about the problem with a culture of fear in security: "If we have a blame culture, a culture of fear, then people don't make fewer mistakes . . . they just don't tell us about them."

Chapter 18

Stealing the Keychain

Y ou may think that my job is super glamorous and like that of a spy, and often it is. I can't deny the benefits—the amazing places I have visited and the incredibly weird and wonderful things I have done, legally, that would put the average citizen in jail. Stealing valuable items and breaking into places is, without a doubt, the most unusual career anyone could have. No one at my school could have predicted I would become a hacker and mastermind of criminal behaviors.

But it isn't always glamorous. There are the odd times when my clients have an interest in protecting what everyone else would call . . . well, let's just say not pleasant.

I grew up near the sea in Essex, England. A place I removed myself from as soon as finances would allow. I am not a fan of the smell, the noises, the smell, or the seagulls. Did I mention the smell? I am not a lover of fish or the smell of fish, so you can imagine my abject horror that one client wanted their fish processing plant assessed.

Raw fish smells horrible, in my opinion. A fish processing plant? Well, that smells like a hot Saturday morning on Bourbon Street in New Orleans, only 10 times worse.

This job was not actually supposed to be a physical assessment; we were there for a simple penetration test of the client's network. But this was one of the few times a client got a physical assessment for free.

The day started off badly. There had been a failure of communication at the company, so they did not expect me and a colleague on site. We were left in a sun-filled glass reception area for two hours with blazing sunshine heating the room while the smell of raw fish permeated our clothes. We were given a small desk and one too few seats, meaning we had to take turns standing.

The access we needed to the server room was a bigger problem. The only person who had access was on vacation, abroad, and wasn't contactable. The day was getting worse, and the smell was now starting to absorb into my skin.

It was at some point during this fish-infused baking that I decided to gain access to the server room myself. With the client's permission, I walked along to the server room to figure out how to break in. Along with a remote access system, there was a key override—I just had to find the key. I hadn't brought my lock-picking kit, as I wasn't planning to use it, and it is illegal in some countries to carry it when it's not for work purposes.

A short while later, I was able to track down the temporary security office in a portable cabin on the outskirts of the site. I stomped over, sweating what I believe was Omega 3 fish oil, and knocked on the cabin door. No answer. Typical.

I tried the cabin door, and it opened; they had left it unlocked! On the wall behind a small plastic desk was the key safe. It was left open, as these things so often are—to help with access, rather than, you know, for the security purposes a key safe is actually made for. I had no patience left, and rather than waste more time figuring out the key I needed in this tiny hot box, I took all the keys.

I figured I would find the key I needed in the somewhat cooler inside of the building rather than in the direct sun. I removed about 20 keys and stuffed them into my pockets. Sounding like a jailer, I walked back to the server room.

After only a couple of tries, we had access to the server room and could perform our rather delayed testing. I blame the heat and lack of time for me not returning the other keys straight away. The server room was at least very cool. If you haven't been in a server room before, you may not be aware that they keep servers cooler than humans, as servers tend to complain more than people and stop working much quicker when they get too hot. As good as the air conditioning was, however, there was a big drawback: it pulled in the smell of freshly processed fish, so the room stank like nothing I want to experience again.

Several hours later, I went back to the security cabin. I saw two security guards looking puzzled and whispering quietly to each other conspiratorially. They watched without saying a word as I strode in, opened the key safe, and proceeded to return all the keys that I had borrowed.

I walked out and nodded to the two guards, who apparently were too shocked to engage with me or to even ask who I was or why I had their keys. I think they were just relieved that they didn't need to explain to their boss how they had lost so many keys in one go.

Chapter 19

It's Dangerous to Go Alone. Take This!

In the 1980s, Nintendo was the gaming console taking the world by storm. *The Legend of Zelda* was a smash hit, with the player taking control of the hero, Link, in hopes of rescuing the princess, Zelda. In the opening parts of the game, an elderly man offers Link his first weapon and utters the famous phrase, "It's dangerous to go alone. Take this!" In my world, the best weapon you have is not a sword but knowledge, and reconnaissance is the most vital part of any assessment. Without knowledge, you will almost certainly fail.

There are many ways to map out a target building. You can do a lot of intelligence gathering before you even turn up on site. Most people will be aware of street view via Google. Some may even know about other resources, such as Bing maps with a similar system. Comparing sites like that can help work out layouts. You can extrapolate a lot of information about how a building is constructed if you understand what needs to be done to make a building shaped the way it is. You can work out entrance points, easily spot fire escapes, and in some cases see through the windows. You can do an incredible amount of work just by looking at street-view images.

But there are other resources. Consider sites like OpenStreetMap and Open Infrastructure Map. I have used these to discover where electricity is provided from and where it enters buildings, once finding my way into a site through a small cabin mapped on OpenStreetMap that lined up with power lines on Open Infrastructure Map. Once inside that small cabin, there were access tunnels into the main building.

I have been known to use photogrammetry to create 3D representations of larger sites. Drones can be invaluable if permitted in the area. But do not take everything you see online as gospel, as due to the nature of some sites, they can be altered by Google. Be sure to visit the place you are going to attack, because what things look like in reality can be drastically different from what is portrayed on the internet.

A great example of this is a location I was at recently. Looking at satellite maps on Google, you would be led to believe it was 1,000 acres of farmland: small buildings are shown, with small roads intersecting fields and houses. But on-site, if you were to visit the area, you would see no farms. Instead, you would see large bunkers: squat, raised concrete buildings, all of them mostly hidden behind a large concrete wall topped with double razor wire. Each bunker is used to store munitions. To the untrained eye, you would barely notice this place, but when you know what they look like, these bunkers stand out! On top of several bunkers are surface-to-air launch systems. Nothing at all like the farms you would expect. I am not saying that if you were targeting a small bank in England's Oxfordshire, it would have the power to convince Google to change the images of what is shown; rather, my point is that the dissonance between internet-based observations and real life can be vast.

One of my favorite methods for gaining intelligence about any building layout is to just get into it. I know that sounds counter to what I've been saying so far: recon, recon, recon, and then enter. Well, there are ways to do recon and enter the building at the same time. A lot of very large organizations are in shared buildings. It is rare, even in smaller cities, to find a single client in one building. The following method is great for organizations that are in a shared building, but it can even work well for clients that occupy a whole building themselves.

If you enter any public area of a building, you will no doubt see what is called a *fireman's map*.

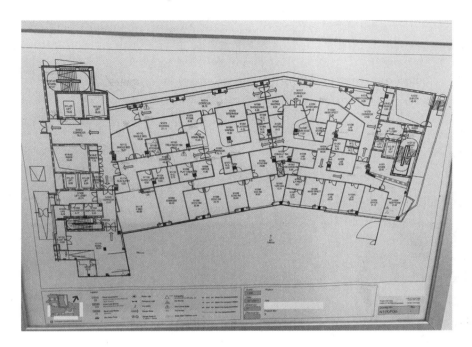

Generally, these are placed in lobbies or entrances to large office buildings. Like most things, now that I have pointed it out, you will see such a map more often: this is called the *Baader-Meinhof phenomenon*, aka *frequency illusion*.

Fireman's maps are there for emergencies. If a fire breaks out, the on-site response teams will have no idea about the layout of the building. They will have no idea where emergency routes are, where water mains run, etc. So, a map is usually easily accessible in case there is a fire and emergency services need to quickly get the lay of the land. You can almost always walk into any large office, take a photo of the map, and walk out without anyone approaching you or asking you why. In some circumstances, you can remove the map, but I really suggest you don't; it is there for a reason, after all.

When you have this map, you have full knowledge of where rooms and, more importantly, hiding places are located. You can work out escape routes and ingress points to secure locations. These maps are a wealth of information and can help you more than any other resource. I have used these maps to locate hidden areas and circumvent security controls. It is important to either take a photo or remember key routes that you may need to escape.

The next time you go into a large office or stay in a hotel room, keep an eye out for maps like this and see if you can find anything interesting.

Chapter 20
The Gold Bar

I am a big fan of movies, so I like to understand what happens behind-the-scenes. Many things in movies are not remotely like reality, and this happens for a lot of reasons. There are those things that are complete fantasy, like an 80-foot dragon. Some are effects meant to appear real, but for the sake of safety or cost, they are faked, like buildings exploding. Some are real effects but carried out under stringent safety rules and so must be augmented, with things like safety wires removed with CGI.

But there is one movie effect I cannot abide: the lack of awareness of just how heavy a gold bar is. I have seen it pulled off sensibly—almost believably, in fact—in only a couple of movies, most notably *Die Hard with a Vengeance*. The weight of your average gold bar (the one that you are no doubt picturing in your mind as you read this) is 12.5 kg or 400 oz.

It is what is known in the finance world as a "Good Delivery Bar." These bars are regulated worldwide and must meet standards set by the London Bullion Market Association.

To be a Good Delivery Bar of gold, the specifications are:
- *Fineness:* Minimum of 995.0 parts per 1,000 fine gold
- *Marks:* Serial number, refiner's hallmark, fineness, year of manufacture
- *Gold content:* 350–430 troy ounces (11–13 kg)
- *Recommended dimensions:*
    - Length (top): 210–290 mm (8.3–11.4 inches)
    - Width (top): 55–85 mm (2.2–3.3 inches)
    - Height: 25–45 mm (0.98–1.77 inches)

As you can tell, it is a very small item, but it weighs as much as a two-and-a-half-year-old child. If you don't have a small child to pick up, pick up a 24-can pack and a 6-pack, which should weigh about 12.5 kg. Not necessarily something you couldn't pick up by yourself, but you're probably not running around with it or throwing it around. You certainly are not going to chuck five or six of them in a backpack and expect them not to rip out the bottom.

I give you all this information not so that you can laugh at movies but to give you a baseline for the assessment I am about to describe. It is one that I have spoken about at many security conferences around the globe throughout the years.

This assessment takes place in London at a large bank. Not the type you normally see on the high street—this is a bullion trading bank. They don't have customers walking in; they don't have much cash on-site, in fact. They have banks of computers, with lots of intelligent people in suits watching graphs and clicking things.

But like any bank, they do keep some reserves, mostly for regulatory reasons. This bank, in particular, had a stash of Good Delivery Bars sitting in a safe that really did look like it was from the movies.

I had been tasked to get inside the building. It was pretty well defended, with good cameras and decent security doors. Exits and other ingress points were monitored, and there were roaming guards around the building and some other little things I won't mention here because I don't want to compromise the other security controls; you'll just have to find them out yourself if you want to break in.

I was able to gain access via a third-party building that I had access to. This wasn't quite via me running a zip line across the rooftops, but not too far off.

Once I had accessed the building, my job was pretty much done, but I had been given a secondary target of trying to access the vault floor.

Vaults are heavy. Very heavy. They are steel-reinforced concrete with incredible technology in the filling: things like cobalt chips to prevent drilling, tremor sensors, and sometimes even glass plates that, if broken, trigger locking mechanisms that can never be undone. Modern bank vaults are a masterpiece of ingenuity and technology. But like all security, given time and money, they can be compromised. I wasn't expecting to do any safe cracking that day, but I had my secondary target, and honestly, I knew just seeing the vault would be incredible.

Because vaults are so heavy, large banks and reserves like this are often built around the vault rather than the vault being placed into an existing structure. The vault is placed on heavy foundations, and the building is then constructed around it. You can't have items such as gold bars on an upper floor; things like safe rooms in the houses of high-net-worth individuals can also cause sagging in a building due to the weight of the materials, even with appropriate reinforcement.

So, I knew that the vault room would be in the basement levels, not on the top floors or even the middle floors with the traders. I made my way downstairs, and after avoiding a couple of security guards, I found myself as low in the building as I could go without entering the drainage systems. I walked along a corridor and into a fairly large open room with a few desks scattered around. It looked more like a storage area than what you would picture for a vault. But there it was. Out in the open, not walled in as expected. Quite frankly, it took me by surprise and looked pretty fake: a large block of metal like one of those hotel safes but 10 feet high and just as square.

I walked around the perimeter of this 10-foot block of metal, and on the south side of the building, opposite what looked to be a loading door, was the main vault entrance.

It was open!

I was gobsmacked. It must be a trap or a ruse or something. When I peered inside, I saw a couple of pallets of perfect gold bars. Each pallet was on a blue pallet mover. I approved of the gold and blue color scheme. But come on, this had to be a trick, right?

I walked into the vault, expecting an alarm to sound or someone to appear and shout at me. I was poised to retrieve my letter of authority. But nothing happened. I waited for what felt like ages, but it was probably a few seconds. I reached out and picked up one of the bars. It was heavy, and I had no bag with me, so I had to cradle it in my arms. I could probably liberate more, but one was enough proof.

From the moment I picked it up, I could tell it was real, and I had just lucked out on literally everything about this heist. One bar was worth about $800,000 at the time of writing this book, and it was maybe half that at the time.

I left the floor as quickly as I could, carrying my new friend. I knew I would be caught if I didn't hide it soon, so I availed myself of a handy rucksack, which I found empty and abandoned in the corner of a meeting room. I carefully placed the bar into the bag with my jacket rolled up around it to protect the bag from sharp corners and hopefully stop the weight from piercing the bag.

Several minutes later, I was strolling out a smokers' exit into an alleyway, constantly expecting someone to accost me. I tried not to look nervous as I escaped around the corner and headed to a nearby café to call my client and debrief them.

It is an understatement to say that the client was shocked and taken aback by everything I told them on the phone. In what seemed like seconds, he was sitting opposite me in the café, out of breath from running.

I opened my backpack and, like an archaeologist unraveling an ancient Egyptian artifact, unwrapped my jacket from the gold bar. As his eyes took in the first glint of gold, both his hands clamped over his mouth to try to stifle a gasp.

We walked back into the building and had an emergency meeting with the highest-seniority people who were in the building at the time: the head of security, the head of reserves, the head of trading, three directors, and two other board members. We sat in a long meeting room, leather-bound black chairs lining the walls, with vast floor-to-ceiling windows on two sides overlooking the London skyline. Once everyone had settled down and introductions were made, without saying anything else, I unceremoniously put my backpack on the huge mahogany table, pulled out my jacket, and unwrapped the bar. The reaction was first shock, then silence—and then you could almost hear thoughts clicking into place as, around the table, a huge uproar broke out.

It turned out that this particular bank had a reputation for being secure, even among other banks. I had singlehandedly and with zero resistance walked into their most secure floor, then into an open vault, removed a gold bar, and left with the bar.

As I have mentioned, debriefs are vital for the client to understand and learn from their mistakes. For this client, I know it took them many years, with many changes in staff and, above all, a huge cultural change, to fix the security issues we highlighted. I also know that since the assessment, it would be much more difficult for anyone to remove any bullion from that bank again.

You may be wondering, as I was at the time, why was the vault door left open? Why were there no guards around? Well, it turns out that I had been incredibly lucky. The day I arrived, an assay was to take place, which is when they check the gold. As part of that assessment, the bank had to conduct its own stock take, make sure all the serial numbers matched what was expected, and, ultimately, check that none of the bars were missing. The clerks doing this had been entering and leaving the vault, and due to time locks, they had followed the procedures laid out and left the door open while they moved in and out and performed their tasks. The security guards were meant to stay with them to make sure any bars they removed went back in.

So, when the clerks had taken two bars out, the security guards went with them. Apparently, making sure two bars didn't go missing was somehow more important than the other few hundred behind the unlocked vault door.

Chapter 21

Plush Carpets

In the corporate world, there is nothing that shows you are making money like renovating a perfectly good office. From complete redesigns to retrofitting, there are a thousand ways to spend a million dollars. The trouble with money is that it rarely buys sense—not just of style, but a sense of how security works.

We have seen in previous chapters that a failure to understand how things work together will almost always result in a failure of security rather than building it up.

More than 20 years ago, I was contracted to work for a well-known high-street bank in the UK. The bank's head offices needed some security testing, and as a leader in the field, I had been requested to go to their headquarters and perform my magic.

It was some time in the autumn of the year, and gaining access to the main building was laughably easy. The smokers huddled around the outside of the building like wildebeests at a watering hole trying to stand close enough to each other to protect themselves. In a large jacket, I was able to mill around the group, despite being a nonsmoker. The herd mentality that smokers have is unwavering, and within seconds I was welcomed into their fold after offering someone a light. It pays to be prepared for situations like this!

As with all groups, there is always a leader, and when that person finished their cigarette and headed toward the door, so did several others. I quietly followed along, and although the leader swiped their ID badge against the door, the rest of us did not. This technique is one of the easiest ways into any building, but remember, it's illegal to do this without permission!

Once inside the building, I was tasked to remove multiple assets. While performing these tasks, I noticed that one particular area of the building was said to be off limits: the directors' offices. These were in a secure area that was restricted and could only be accessed via one double-wide security door.

I was ultimately able to remove some very interesting documents from these offices. When my client inquired how I gained access and was able to move freely in and out, I decided to take them down to the security doors in question and show them why that area was in no way restricted.

We walked down to the main crossroad in the building and headed toward the directors' wing. I strode several steps ahead and pushed the security door open. I turned to see the client and his entourage staring at me as if I had just performed a magic trick and made an elephant appear.

I invited them into the wing and showed them the amazing redecorations going on: the new wood-panelled corridors, the fancy chairs, and the lovely brass plaques. The entire wing of the building that housed several directors was being renovated; multiple offices were hidden under plastic, and most of the office contents were still there in boxes.

After this, I stood in front of them and bounced gently on my toes. "What do you think of the lovely new carpet?" The client and entourage did similarly, and nods of approval were accompanied by a few grunts of appreciation. "Great—now look at what their money bought them!" I said, as I walked over to the security door and flung it wide open.

The plush new carpet, almost half an inch thick, with a gaudy pattern bolstered underneath by an expensive foam underlay, stuck up past the bottom of the security door by a quarter of an inch. The thick fibers scraped under the door as the heavy spring did its best to fight the friction and shut the door. Just an inch or two before closing, it lost its fight, and the security door stood ajar—no locking mechanism was able to overcome the gap. Thanks to the expensive carpet, the door would not and could not close. Even when pushed shut, the fibers gathered at the edge and prevented the door from ever fully closing.

I was astonished that no one had spotted that the door never shut. I often wonder about that client and wish I had followed up to learn what their solution to this issue was. Did they remove the carpet, which would have cost tens of thousands, or did they replace the doors at a huge expense? Who knows? They probably just assumed that the carpet would wear down eventually.

I think this is a great example of why security should always be involved in any project. The day rate of a security consultant such as myself at first looks incredibly expensive, but when you consider the cost to retrofit the office after the fact, the costs of expertise diminish rapidly. Doors are tricky to get right. Throughout my career, doors have been the most misconfigured security measure I see. There are several other stories about them in this book, and I am sure I will be writing about doors for years to come.

Chapter 22
Clean(er) Access

It's the end of an assessment, and I'm doing the walkaround with the client, which involves taking the client around the building and pointing out all the flaws and insecurities that leave them vulnerable to attack. To prove that I've accessed areas I shouldn't have been able to, I leave stickers or take photos.

During this walkaround, I take the CSO to the basement of the building, which is being renovated. When we get there, it's deserted, and his swipecard won't allow access to the floor. I convince him we should hang around for a few minutes, although he doesn't really see the point. Just as he is getting impatient, the door to the floor opens, and a cleaner comes through.

Spotting me, she greets me warmly: "Oh, hiya! Back again?"

"Hi love, yeah—last time I'll be back today. Can you just hold the door for us so I can show my colleague?"

And in we go. The floor is deserted and half-renovated, with bits of floorboard and ceiling yet to be put in place. The CSO acknowledges that I got into a floor I shouldn't have been able to but can't work out why it matters, when nothing is there. I ask him how he knows that nothing is there, and he looks at me like I'm an idiot, stretching his arm out wide and saying, "Look! There's nothing here! No desks, no people, no filing cabinets or computers!"

"But there will be people here soon, right?" I ask.

"Well, yes," he says, still in that you're-an-idiot voice. "When the floor's laid, and the ceiling's in place, there will be people working here."

"So that open floor would be the perfect place for me to put a bug, don't you think?"

"Oh. Yeah. . ." He suddenly doesn't look or sound quite as confident as he did moments before.

"Not to mention all the places I could have hidden in here today, waiting until the rest of the building was empty so that I could have the whole place to myself."

"Yeah—I get it now."

The client was slow on the uptake about why empty or under-renovation areas are a key security vulnerability, and I shouldn't have been surprised. I have a very skewed view of the world, and even security professionals like the client do not cross over into the murky world of espionage.

So, for those of you who are not in the espionage business, it might be a little confusing as to why this anecdote matters. In the world of large corporations such as this one, industrial espionage is rife. *Espionage* is just a fancy word for when one entity spies on another. In this case, large corporations have been known to spy on competitors to understand what their businesses are going to be doing—will they be bringing a new product to market that will outsell or diminish profits? Maybe the company is about to do something that may affect stock prices, and the company spying on it might be able to use that foreknowledge to make huge amounts of money. I would love to go into more detail about corporate and even government espionage, but that would be an entire book on its own.

In this case, the ability to gain access to a floor that was being renovated was a fantastic opportunity for an expert to place long-life bugs: these are bugs that are wired for electricity instead of using batteries. In a similar case, an Embassy was found to have bugs embedded in the walls and underfloor cavities, each one wired into the building electrical system. Due to their locations, this could only have happened during construction and not after.

Chapter 23

What We Do
in the Shadows

My job takes me to some incredible locations. Due to a fear of heights I didn't set foot onto a plane until I was 40, but since then, I have been flown around the world by clients to over 20 countries, put up in luxury five-star hotels, and had the pleasure of waiting things out beside turquoise seas while sipping non-alcoholic cocktails as the sand warms my feet.

But that is more the exception than the rule. People often think that my work is non-stop fun, and while that can be true in some circumstances, there is a lot of paperwork to be done! I get requests all the time from colleagues or strangers asking if I can take them along on jobs. Maybe they want the thrill of it, or maybe they want to get a job doing what I do. I almost always have to say no due to client sensitivity, but now and then I have been able to bring some colleagues along on an assessment.

On one particular recon mission, I brought a colleague along. It was the dead of night in a big city. We parked nearby and crept around the perimeter of the building. The flash exterior of the entrance was just for show; the boring grey brickwork on the other sides of the building was much more appealing to me.

We took about an hour to walk the entire perimeter, making sure we were not picked up by CCTV and that we did not look suspicious to anyone who could see us. After a quick recon mission, my colleague assumed we were done and was already getting sore feet. We had just started. I vaulted over a short iron fence with those little spikes on it: it had been painted over so many times that no one was going to get hurt by them.

We both got over, and I lifted up an access panel; at this point, I could tell my colleague was a little hesitant, but once I was in, he had to follow. We found ourselves in a series of pitch-black tunnels. I used the light on my phone as a small flashlight, and we walked forward and, most concerningly, downward. The tunnels under this site were extensive. I had seen them on plans, but I am not sure the plans captured the level we were now on. The moldy stench and stillness of the air said to me that no one went down there, at least not very often. I started to worry that there might not be a way into the main building from here. We started to get to larger corridors, still damp to our feet. Either the smell subsided, or I had gotten used to it.

We came across some pretty grim areas down there. I managed to take a photograph of one room that was half bricked up and flooded.

It's hard to see in the picture, but the water must have been three or four feet deep, and detritus floated around the stagnant pool. My colleague was getting jittery. He commented that it was starting to feel a little like the Blair Witch might attack us. I had never considered how dangerous and lonely such a job could be. Anyone or anything could be hidden down here; it occurred to me that abandoned and unkept areas are always places that attract criminals. I spent a lot of my childhood hiding in dark, unreachable places to keep safe, so I hadn't really thought to be concerned, but it was wrecking the nerves of my friend. I decided we had to get somewhere better lit.

We eventually found our way upward, and a few emergency low-level lights appeared. We kept walking toward more of the lights.

Suddenly, we thought we could hear noises up ahead. Sounds do funny things in small corridors, so we hunched down, listening and waiting. We crept around and saw a white door with a faded Exit sign hung above it. We decided to exit the building and come back later. My colleague rushed forward: with the apparent end in sight, he embraced his need to escape. He lurched forward and swung the door open into the cold crisp morning air.

That's when things went a bit wrong. A squat round figure blocked his path, silhouetted against the glow of the sodium lights. My colleague screamed as though he had seen the Hound of the Baskervilles, and I saw him swing his fist at the shadowy "monster." I was able to prevent the hit from landing on the shocked guard, who was just on a sneaky smoke break and was as startled by our sudden appearance as we were by his. I dragged my friend into the street, still swearing and shouting, and we ran until our hearts pounded and lactic acid burned our legs. We were in a park, where we collapsed on the damp grass. Somehow, we had outrun the security guard.

I had to wait some time before I could get into that building on my own due to the security guard being spooked and reporting vagrants in the area. The emergency exit door was secured, but the original access panel was not. It turned into a remarkably successful assessment, but my colleague never wanted to do my job again.

Chapter 24

What Do I Know about Diamonds?

A ctually, more than I ever could have imagined while growing up in poverty. Little did I know then that I would perform diamond heists (legally) as part of my job—once I even got locked into a diamond warehouse by accident. Some of my most incredible anecdotes took place in areas I am not allowed to talk about. Although I can sometimes hint at certain aspects or omit parts for the sake of security, the unfortunate truth is that the best complete anecdotes will never see the light of day.

This chapter focuses on a specific security system at a nondescript building hidden in the heart of England. But before we begin, I need to give you a little background. Often, the people who hire us to do this type of work do not work on-site, which can lead to animosity. Some people view my work as an attack on their work, especially those in charge of security or who have security as part of their role. This is the opposite of what I am there to do (my aim is simply to improve security), but it is human nature to dislike what we perceive as a threat.

In this case, the head of security met me after I had already circumvented the building's initial perimeter—I greeted him in the reception area rather than waiting for him at the fence line. This had already put him in a bad mood, because he realized that his security might not be up to scratch. He was about to go from annoyed to furious.

During the security check-in, I was directed toward a capsule. You may never have seen one of these tubes: they are called *man traps*, and they have that name for a reason. A person enters the tube from one side and is shut into it. Once security is satisfied to let them in, the door opens on the other side of the tube, and the person can walk into the secure side of the barrier.

This particular site housed some very precious items. Search and screen policies were in place for items such as bags, but people were sneaky and could hide items around their bodies in interesting places. For this reason, the man-trap tubes had an extra feature: they could weigh you.

Here's how this works. A person coming into the facility is weighed fairly accurately, and their weight is recorded. When they leave, they are weighed again by the same tube. Any differences could indicate stolen items being smuggled. (Before you wonder about body waste during the day, there were no toilets on the secure side of the facility; people had to leave to relieve themselves and then be reweighed.)

This was the first time I had seen one of these weighing man-traps in use, and I hope you can see the design flaw that quickly occurred to me. I stepped into the tube and turned to face the security guy. I then performed a star jump, holding myself against the sides of the tube so I looked like the Vitruvian Man wedged in a pipe. A look of shock and confusion ran across the security guy's face, which turned into rage as he realized what I was doing. The tube recorded my weight not in hundreds of pounds but in single digits.

If I performed a similar feat on the way out, I could have millions of dollars' worth of items stashed around my body without the weight changing. Obviously, someone would notice if I jumped as high as I did, but they would not see me doing so subtly a few inches off the ground.

I stepped out of the tube onto the secure side of the barrier. I watched as the ball of rage waited impatiently for the tube to reset itself, let him in, weigh him, and then allow him to explode from the other side into my face. As this is a book that might be read by young adults, I will not recount here his fine words of appreciation for my technique.

During my assessments, I am not there to make people feel stupid or threatened. I know it's often easier to identify flaws than to fix them. But I am there to highlight security concerns, and one of the biggest mistakes I see is the assumption that cost equals security. Even the most expensive systems can be bypassed if they are not created, installed, and used correctly. Throughout this book, you will see many examples, with ultra-expensive doors, biometrics, and Hollywood-style security systems being bypassed because of the lack of understanding about their place in security.

Chapter 25

How to Crack a Safe

It all looks so easy, doesn't it? You watch a movie or TV show. During the build-up, they recruit the usual suspects: a getaway driver (or wheelman, as they are called in the industry), a mastermind, a computer nerd, an ex-soldier, and, somewhere in the group, a safecracker. He is there to do one job: get into the safe! Inevitably he will, and generally, the story calls for him to be shot or otherwise taken out. I see no sense in taking out the one person who can't be replaced easily, but I digress. Safe cracking is an art form, but like everything in life, it is a skill that can be learned.

There are many types of safes: for example, those awfully insecure hotel safes with a four-digit PIN and a key bypass that can be opened many ways, even with a swift thump on the top or side. Those safes can also be carried away if not secured correctly.

Then you have slightly better safes: they might have one of those fancy dials you see in the movies and are generally very heavy and bolted to a wall or a floor. There are also hidden versions, underneath floorboards or a painting in an office. This happens more than you'd imagine. I know a mayor's office in Essex, England, that has one, for example.

Then you have the huge safes you can walk into: room-sized vaults that have multiple locking systems and a myriad of defenses and look imposing.

But as I am sure you have learned from this book, everything is a compromise between usability and security. Safes and vaults are built to be used. And when there is a way in, there is always a way to compromise them.

I am going to try to teach you the mechanism of cracking a safe. It's one I have used over the years, and it's more complicated and tricky than you probably hope. It's not just sitting with your ear to the safe door and twiddling the dial. Well, not all the time.

We cover lock picking and digital bypasses elsewhere in this book, so in this chapter we are going to focus on dial locks. Here is what the external section of the lock looks like. You've likely seen a lock like this—maybe not in real life but at least in a TV show or movie. The part you can see is called the *combination dial* for obvious reasons—it's where you enter the combination.

Inside are *wheels* that together make the *wheel pack*. The combination dial attaches to a spindle that runs through the wheel pack and attaches to the drive cam. The lock also has a fence, drive pins, and a wheel notch, but we will get to those in a moment.

The number of wheels in the pack determines how many numbers are in the combination. Three wheels, three numbers. Four wheels, four numbers. So far, pretty simple.

When you turn the combination dial, the spindle turns the drive wheel, and the drive pin attached to that wheel hits the nearest wheel at a specific point that corresponds to the correct first number. This is known as *picking up* because as the combination dial moves, so does the picked-up wheel. Note that this happens from back to front: the wheel farthest from the dial is the first number, and the nearest to the dial is the last number. Each wheel has a driver pin and picks up the wheel in front when the combination is entered.

Once all the wheels have been picked up, they are aligned. There is a notch in every wheel. If the wheels are picked up in the correct place (the combination is correct), the holes line up, too. This allows the *fence*, which is just a long bar, to fall into the gap. This gets the bar out of the way of the bolt, which is holding the door shut.

In summary, you turn the dials the correct way to open a gap in the wheels to allow the fence to drop and the bolt to slide back so you can open the safe.

It may take some mental agility to visualize what's happening, but re-read and look at the photos again to picture the process.

Combination locks like this often have a left, right, left combination due to the way wheels are picked up. Some safes start leftward, and some start right. But with practice, you can figure out which is the correct way.

Cracking can happen in a few forms. Before starting, you have to reset the wheels. You do this by spinning the combination dial several times one way to release all the wheels.

The first way to open this type of safe is pretty simple; literally everyone can do it. It's called *brute forcing*: guessing every combination you can. It sounds daunting, but it can be incredibly simple and effective.

Start with right 0, left 0, right 0. Then try opening the lock. Reset and try right 1, left 0, right 0. Sounds boring, I know. But if you have a three-number combination using 0–9, you only need to try 720 times, and you are guaranteed to guess the code eventually. The same is true for a dial combination safe, bike lock, or gym locker. If the lock uses four numbers 0–9, that's trickier: you need to guess 10,000 times! Given enough time, you could get into any safe this way. But in most cases, you don't have enough time and will get caught.

There must be a smarter way. You can reduce the number of guesses by picking sensible combinations and removing unlikely ones. Who would set their safe to 0.0.0 or 9.9.9? You should try simple ones like 1.2.3. and 0.0.7., though. You may get lucky. Four-digit combinations are often significant dates that people can remember.

This is one of the reasons we security folks tell people to choose PINs that are not dates! Don't use 1225 or 0911 or 0101, or even 3111, all of which are significant dates.

Proper safes can have 0–99 numbers and up to six wheels in their pack. I would print out the extraordinarily long number of combinations you would need to try, but my editor might think I was padding this book! It's a very big number; even if you tried one combination every second, you couldn't try all them combinations even after years.

If brute forcing won't work, what will? No point in being destructive. There are mechanisms in most safes to prevent or at least significantly slow down physical forced entry. Even the most basic safe can take more than half an hour of drilling, and even then, other security measures might kick in, let alone the noise involved.

The only method left is learning to *crack* the safe.

But try one thing before you try to crack your newly found safe: try opening the door. More businesses than I can count have failed at this step. A safe is safe when it is locked. However, putting in the combination every time is a hassle, and a lot of businesses (even diamond centers) that use a safe frequently keep it on what is known to safecrackers as *day lock*. This means the owner entered the combination at the start of the day and then just shuts the door. Sometimes they leave the last digit to be entered. Best case, the safe is unlocked. It only needs to be opened. Worst case, you need to guess one number. Honestly, I have opened more safes than you would believe just by trying the door.

OK, so you have tried the door, and it's locked. The numbers 0–99 are on the dial, and the safe has between four and six wheels. What now?

In 1940, Harry C. Miller came up with a method for cracking safes like this. It's broken down into three fairly simple steps:

1. Determine the contact points.
2. Figure out the number of wheels in the wheel pack.
3. Graph your results.

Let's go over these steps and what they mean.

The notches in the wheel are shaped in a way to allow the lever and fence to pass through when the wheel comes around. When the nose of the lever makes contact with the slope, there is a faint click. A stethoscope or a keen ear will definitely help you! By listening for these clicks, you can work out where the contact area is. In our case, let's say it's between the numbers 10 and 20.

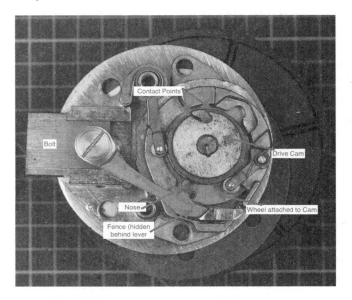

The key is to dial the number opposite that contact area; let's say it's between 60 and 70. Dialing that in is called *parking the wheels*. Now, if you keep spinning the combination dial the same way, you will hear another faint click as the wheels pick up another wheel. The number of clicks you hear determines the number of wheels you have.

You have the contact point and the number of wheels, so you are already mostly done!

Reset the lock by turning the wheel several times. This allows you to pick up all the wheels and park them at 0 (not the 60 we used earlier).

You also need to create your graphs. Two-line graphs are best for this: the X-axis goes left to right, and the Y-axis goes up and down.

Each graph's X-axis should go from 0 to the largest number on the combination dial: in our case, 99. The Y-axis only needs to cover a few numbers. Make two of these graphs.

Label one graph's X-axis *Starting Position* and its Y-axis *Left Contact Point.*

Label the second graph's X-axis *Starting Position* and its Y-axis *Right Contact Point.*

Now turn the dial very slowly to the left, and listen for the sound of the contact points; you are listening for *two* clicks. To graph the contact points, on your Left Contact Point graph, mark a point where X=0 (where you started) and Y is the number where you heard the first click. On the Right Contact Point graph, mark a point where X=0 and Y is the number of the second click.

Repeat this process, but park the wheels three numbers left of 0: on a 0–99 wheel, that means parking at 97. This will be the new X you mark on your graphs. Keep repeating and graphing the contact points. Each time you do this, the contact points will shift.

The graph will show a convergence at the numbers used in the combination of the safe. It's easier to overlay both graphs to see this or use two color pens on the same graph.

You now have all the numbers but not the order. For example, suppose the safe uses the combination 7, 21, 95, 42, 5. The graph will show the numbers.

You still have to brute force those!

7,21,95,42,5

5,42,95,21,7

7,42,21,5,95

and so on.

There are caveats to this process, as always. For example, we park every three numbers because most safes give a margin of error. Higher-end safes are more accurate, so you need to graph more accurately and try parking every number.

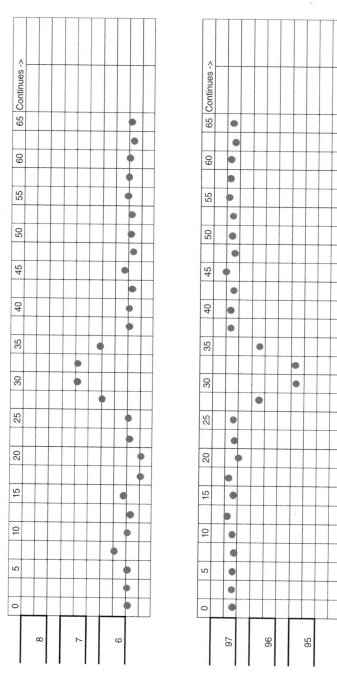

Graphs for illustration purposes

This is not a book on safe cracking—there are already many of those and countless YouTube videos—but I wanted to give you a taste of how it's done and show you that it is possible. If you want to get into this hobby, I recommend watching some videos and maybe even buying a few cheaper safes to practice on.

I hope you now have an idea of how to crack a safe. Not only is it a very cool skill, but you'll be able to pick faults with heist movies to impress your friends.

Chapter 26

Find a Safe Space

We have covered how to crack a safe, but where do you find one? They are not just lying around . . . right? Well, honestly, you will be shocked by how many safes you do find lying around.

On many occasions, I have been asked to gain access to sensitive information or valuable assets that were held in a safe. Often, I am not told where that safe is. Finding it may be part of the assessment, and ultimately, a lot of clients don't even expect me to get into their building, let alone find the asset they have tasked me with. Despite my having a 100% success rate (ridiculous but true), clients that want a social engineering or physical assessment generally assume they have finally built a secure site. They keep their cards to their chest and share barely anything with me. Why would they?

I have found safes in all sorts of weird and wonderful places. People think they are smart when hiding safes, but the truth is that most of us think in a similar way. That's why passwords are often easy to deduce, and it's why social engineering is—unfortunately—so easy to do.

When it comes to safes, there are really only a few places you can hide a large metal box. It's not going to be in a wall if the wall is four inches thick. It's unlikely to be installed in the floor if the office is not on the ground floor, because the floor is too thin or weak to hold a safe.

When you start to consider the limitations of where you can fit this heavy metal box, you also understand that people with safes love to open them regularly. If we think about an office, it wouldn't be practical to hide a safe behind a heavy bookshelf that needs two people to move it and maybe has delicate glassware on the shelves. With this mindset, we can rule out a lot of locations.

As with all security, you have to understand the mechanism and the person using it to be able to bypass it in the easiest manner.

Hidden drawers in desks are a reality, and they are almost never as cool and clever as you read about or see on TV. They are obvious and hideously easy to break into. You just need to sit in the chair, and you will see it. One drawer slightly shorter or heavier, an odd bit of wood color here or there: the tell-tale signs are hard to disguise.

Using paintings on walls is also a reality. A quick glance at the wall, a swift knock with a fist to determine if the wall is solid enough to be a contender, and then a gentle nudge of the corner of each painting will quickly find one of these.

You have obviously large vaults, which are insanely heavy—essentially, large metal and concrete rooms. You won't find these on roofs or higher floors as their weight will not allow it. They are often on the lowest floors and usually built directly on the foundations of the building, with the building then constructed around them. Some ex-banks turned into bars make a feature of the vault just because it is impossible to remove without destroying the building. Such vaults are also pretty cool.

In between the hidden office safe and the large vaults, you have the mid-range safe, the type you see in small-end shops or larger commercial offices like law firms: a few feet high and weighing enough to prevent two large people from walking off with it. These are hard to hide and become burdensome when doing any renovation or redecorating of an office. Of course, they stick out like sore thumbs and are almost always left where they were first installed, sometimes decades earlier.

When thinking of safes, one of the many times I broke into a building via a basement entrance springs to mind. The entrance was not particularly secure; it had a small padlock that probably would have broken if you looked at it strongly enough. Getting past the lock was trivial. Once in the building, I made my way into the semi-dark basement and wandered around a number of corridors until as I was heading towards the loading bay I eventually found my way to a storage room in the basement. It was wide and well lit, and it appeared that the company just used it as an occasional storage area.

I found boxes of Christmas decorations, a few old desks, and half-broken office chairs—nothing really worth putting into long-term storage and also nothing wanted on the main floors of the office. A purgatory of equipment, I was surprised it wasn't labeled Room 101, like the room containing your worst nightmares from the George Orwell novel '1984'. I walked around the weird-shaped room and kept to the edge to ensure that I had covered it all. That's when I saw it. Discarded in a corner was a safe, looking as if it had been abandoned like an unwanted birthday present, much like the rest of the items in this room. I assumed it was not used; why would it be?

The first shock to me: it was locked. I tried to move it, but it would not budge even a bit. To my surprise, it was either bolted to the floor or insanely heavy. Either way, now I knew I had to get inside it.

I spent some time on this safe, maybe more than I would like to publicly admit, until eventually I was able to open it. What treasures awaited me inside? A lot of paperwork, some petty cash, and a few receipts. It's not always like Indiana Jones, but I was able to take a few photographs and prove to the client that I had been in the safe.

It turned out that this safe was their only safe, and (as you may have guessed from some of my earlier comments about safes being hard to move) it had been installed before they moved in and gutted that room. No one had ever even tried to move it somewhere more sensible, so it just sat there. As the room was only infrequently used for the odd paperwork trip, I could have been down in that "Room 101" for hours or even days without anyone being any the wiser. Luckily, although it took me longer than I would have liked to crack that safe, it wasn't so long that I needed my sleeping bag.

The moral of this story is that if you keep an eye out and think like your target, you never know when or where you might come across a safe!

Chapter 27

Well, That Was Unexpected

Every now and then, something happens that disrupts the entire process. Usually this is when someone down the chain of command has fundamentally misunderstood the role we play in security with our assessments. Through either stupidity or arrogance, and generally a frightening combination of the two, they have no idea what they are doing and have somehow risen to a position of power that is frankly bewildering to me.

Occasionally these individuals ruin everything, and while that is a little annoying, what annoys me more is that they have single-handedly wasted weeks of work and tens of thousands of pounds of our clients' money.

As always, this situation starts with a client approaching us to test the security of a building, often a new building. Let's say it's not meant to be superbly secure, but some sensitive information is contained in some of the offices, so it needs to be security-checked.

With assessments like this, we spend several days performing recon. In this particular case, we unfortunately had to rely on a lot of internet sources due to the remote location. Visiting the site in person could alert security. It was decided that we would do the final recon work on the ground the night before.

During our recon phase, we were introduced to an individual we shall call Bob. Bob was the manager of the building and was reticent about the whole process: my client, the one commissioning the work, worked at a higher level than Bob, so Bob just had to put up with it. Bob also had what we call "slopey shoulders," meaning he didn't want to do any work himself and brushed it off to subordinates.

Several weeks after the internet-based recon, it was time for the on-site assessment. I caught a train and then got a hired car to the site. I staked out the premises in the afternoon, during the evening, and into the night. The place was quiet. When I say quiet, I do not mean 20 or so people. I don't even mean three or four people. I mean dead quiet. No one was around, no lights, nothing. However, it was a Sunday, so I considered that perhaps this location was not in operation on the weekends. This would be surprising, given what the organization does, but I couldn't rule it out.

Monday morning rolled around, and I got to the site around 9:00 a.m., expecting office workers to be coming into the building. I saw nothing; it was still dead as anything. I decided to get a closer look and jumped over a smallish fence and into the grounds. I looked around and through a few windows and saw nothing at all. I hopped back over the fence and went to my car, which I had parked in a hidden spot down the road. I called up my client, who was as perplexed as I was. He said he would have Bob, the slopey-shouldered manager, call me as soon as possible.

Several minutes went by, followed by several more minutes. After about half an hour of nothing, my phone rang, and a flustered young lady began speaking rapidly to me. "Bob just called me and said you were waiting to get into the building. I've been working from home like the rest of us; I wasn't expecting anyone to come to the building because of security. I'll be there in five minutes; I'm so sorry!" She hung up before I could even begin to process what she had just said. With a squeal of tires, she arrived and ran over to the front door. I watched her from behind a wall as she called my phone.

"Where are you? I've just unlocked the door."

I walked over to the entrance and went in. As she spoke to me, the pieces of what had happened started to fall into place. During our brief conversation, she said that I was "welcome to look around the place, but it hasn't been opened yet; no one was allowed to work here until security checked it out. You're that security, aren't you?"

I didn't have the heart to explain the situation from my side. I looked around and took notes that I then fed back to the client.

It turned out that Bob had been put in charge of getting this office up and running and had been feeding his bosses white lies about the current state. To find out their new building was well behind schedule was a bit of a shock to the client.

Security assessments are fantastic for highlighting the dissonance between the expected and the reality of security, whether physical or digital security. But in this case, the poor client was more shocked than most to find such a large gap between what had been going on and what their board was being told.

This is the first and only time to date that I have been handed the keys to a secure building that I was supposed to attack. Having the keys makes the job a bit too easy and a waste of time and money for our client. I guess this shows that sometimes there is a huge disconnect between what people think security is about and what it actually entails. By handing me the keys, the staff undermined the purpose of the assessment. It felt like Bob, with his lack of understanding or care about security, should have been briefed and educated about it.

It's important to understand that security is not just the job of security teams but the responsibility of everyone in the company. And, it is the company's responsibility to empower, motivate, and educate everyone to understand that.

Chapter 28

Opening a Door on Security

I often say that putting security measures in place without understanding the context can make overall security worse. This confuses some people. How can having more security cause less security? I hope that some of the other recollections in this book have given you a little insight into what that means now. There are occasions when people designing buildings or installing controls just have no idea how security should work. I have helped many companies understand their poor security choices after they have made them, but I really like it when we can help those in the initial design and build phases catch issues before they become either too expensive or simply too impractical to rectify.

I wish I had been involved in the building in the following story from the very beginning. To me, it optimizes the point I am trying to make in this book: security should be considered from the start.

Picture a building, a secure one. Even a secure building has two distinct areas. The most valuable secure section (often referred to as the *high side*) is generally off limits to everyone who is not authorized to be there. The other section is less secure (the *low side*). The low side is often the area where visitors are brought into the building and where deliveries are made. Obviously, different organizations and buildings have variations of the security levels. To gain access to the low side, for example, you would not expect to just walk into a government facility if you were a member of the public, but you would for a high street bank.

This delineation between the high and low sides of the building is there for a reason, and the reason is security. When planners, architects, and builders get involved without considering security, it can be really problematic. Let me explain how one such client with a high side and a low side to their building spent millions decking out the extraordinary décor of the offices—but security got totally lost along the way.

I arrived on site for a meeting to discuss a project with this client. I was shown through the public entrance and into the low-side reception area, all as expected. Sitting in a black leather Barcelona chair, I took in the reception space.

To my right was a large black marble reception desk. The floor was made of slate grey polished concrete. To the left of the reception desk were three glass-fronted meeting rooms. Each meeting room had a frosted glass bar across the midway point that gave some sense of privacy but allowed me to see that it was empty. To the left of the rooms was a single elevator with no security mechanism in place—a security issue of its own. I made a note to let the client know at the end of the meeting.

I got lost in my own thoughts for a while until a gentleman opened one of the meeting room doors, giving me a bit of a surprise. Hadn't the room just been empty? Maybe I had missed him. After pleasantries, he ushered me into the meeting room, and then I saw it: the other door.

I was unable to contain myself. I had to investigate. Neither door was protected from either side to prevent it from being opened. I was aghast in horror and explained to the client that anyone could walk in off the street and past reception and enter a meeting room. From there, they could open the other door and enter the high side of the building, all without any badge or key system to authenticate who they were or why they were there.

It had apparently never crossed anyone's mind that they were essentially building an insecure corridor that bypassed all security controls. Never once had they considered that someone could or would do this. The apparent reason for this oversight was the classic case of too many people being involved in the design and building of the interior. I often see this: architects not understanding security, builders not installing security products correctly, and clients making changes to either budgets or design at the last minute. Almost always too late do they get someone like me, a security expert, involved. With almost every project, whether it is a digital project or a physical one, the sooner security experts are brought in, the cheaper it is to fix the issue.

This is what I mean by understanding the whole security ecosystem of a building. If I had asked the security team at this building what measures they had in place, they would have recounted all the right things: a high side with security controls to protect it from the low side. But they would have overlooked the meeting rooms, which bypassed all of their controls, because they just didn't think about the whole system from an attacker's perspective.

Chapter 29

How to Tailgate an Opaque Door

Tailgating is one of the core techniques for breaking into places. In this context, *tailgating* is simply following someone into an entrance. Whether knowingly or not, you have probably done this yourself, either holding the door open for someone following you or requesting that someone hold a door open for you. This can be used to bypass security controls by tricking someone into letting you through an entrance that you don't have legitimate access to.

This can happen in two directions: you either follow someone in the same direction they are traveling, or you enter when they leave.

Performing this technique is incredibly easy when you are following someone, as you can see when they are going to open the door, which makes timing your lunge for the door handle easy. If there is a door you want to get through, you can make yourself look busy: for example, pretending to use your phone while you wait for someone you can follow. The same can be done with a door that is being opened toward you when a person is exiting; however, it can be more challenging. This is especially the case when the door is not used very often or is opaque and you cannot see when someone is about to approach the door.

There is a method I have created for using this technique against an opaque or infrequently used door, and I'm going to share it with you now.

Approach the door you wish to enter and stand to the side of the door, roughly a pace away from it. Reach out with your hand

and grab the door handle. Do not attempt to turn or manipulate it in any way. Now listen carefully for anyone approaching from the other side. You may not be able to hear anything, and you may have to wait a while. You must be ready to react instantly, though.

If someone is heard approaching the door from within or starts to turn the handle, immediately grab the door and pull/push it and step forward. You are aiming to time this to shock the person on the other side. They will almost always think you unlocked the door just before them and it was a coincidence that they were leaving at the same time. The trick here is to sell the fact that you already had access and they were the ones late at opening the door. As always, be polite and confident, not aggressive. Apologize, and hold the door open for them. This psychological trick will make them feel less aggressive toward you while allowing you to control the door and giving you access to the entrance.

I have used this trick in many assessments, and timing is crucial, as is your selling of the situation. This little trick works because of that awkward dance that we, as humans, naturally do when meeting someone this way. Leaning into the awkwardness with a chuckle and an apology is what sells this, making it seem like you belong there and preventing the other person from questioning what you are doing.

This comes into play even more when dealing with single-person turnstiles or speed lanes (the glass barriers that are used as access controls in many buildings). Running into these and "accidentally" turning them into a two-person system creates a very awkward situation that flusters almost everyone. When people feel a bit awkward, they generally prefer to quickly resolve a situation and remove themselves from it, rather than create a fuss and draw attention.

Chapter 30

The Guard Who Was Too Polite

Every now and then, something happens on a job that messes things up a little. These situations don't ruin the job, but they are annoying and require a cool head. This was one such job.

I had tailgated my way into a building. The large open space beyond the door was an atrium of at least three or four stories high, and the grand marble flooring stretched out in a giant square. On one edge was the entrance I had just come in on. To either side were large banks of speed lanes; and opposite me, about 40 feet away, stood a reception desk behind which was a security guard. I could immediately tell that he was very attentive. He had seen me enter, and I could sense that he was watching where I was going to go. I quickly concluded that I couldn't attack the speed lanes under his watchful eye, but I couldn't approach the desk either.

Thankfully, this company had built its entranceway out of glass, so I was able to prepare somewhat for what to expect when I entered the building. I had my mobile phone in my hand and against my ear. As I entered the building, I pretended to be having a very animated call with someone. The security guard watched me as I paced up and down, sometimes dangerously toward the speed lanes on the right but swerving back just as his attention peaked and he was ready to pounce. This went on for some time, well over 10 minutes. I managed to keep myself out of earshot and kept feinting toward the right bank of entrances.

After almost 15 minutes of watching me, the guard eventually got bored and returned to his work behind the reception desk.

Almost immediately he turned around and started working on whatever he had to do. I wasted no time, as I felt that this could be a fleeting opportunity. Within moments, I cleared the speed-lane gate and was casually walking up the wide-open staircase to his left. I positioned myself next to someone as they walked up, too, making it look like we were together in case the eagle-eyed guard glanced up.

Once out of sight, I observed him from over the barrier. I saw him look around before he obviously assumed that I had gone through the right-hand bank of speed lanes. He strained to look for me down that side of the building. Ultimately, he seemed to decide that, as he could no longer see me, I was no longer a threat.

Many hours later, the assessment had drawn to a close, and I was performing a wash-up meeting with the client. I happened to be taken to the reception area, and it was here that the security guard exclaimed, rather loudly, that he had, in fact, seen me as a threat and felt he should be commended for doing so. However, his ego was soon deflated when he was questioned about why he never approached me or tried to find me. His response?

"Well, I was suspicious of him, but he was on a call, so I didn't want to disturb him. I wasn't going to be impolite and interrupt him!"

And when questioned why he didn't try to look for me when I disappeared?

"Well, if he had gone outside, he wasn't a problem, and if he was inside, he must have had a pass and wasn't a problem."

This is what makes social engineering so powerful. We are hard-wired to be polite in some cultures more than others. Lots of organizations have a hierarchy, and if you're dressed in a suit or appear to be in a more senior position, the authority bias will often prevent people from challenging you.

Beyond that, people don't expect the unexpected. Most days run pretty much like the days before them. So, the security guard didn't feel he could confront one of his colleagues (who appeared busy and important) because it just didn't feel culturally or socially appropriate. And it didn't occur to him that someone would jump over the knee-high barriers, simply because it had never happened before.

Chapter 31
The Swan Effect

I love telling this story because it shows the absurdity that is common in security while also highlighting how, in this job, you have to adapt on the spot in tricky situations.

This was some time ago when I was working for another company, just building my skills and trying to show clients the benefits of such assessments.

I had been unable to go to the site physically and perform any of my normal recon, work that is vital to understanding the layout, the employees, and the patterns of life that are so critical to finding security flaws.

Often, during recon, I would be fortunate enough to gain access to an employee's security pass. Many times, I would sit and stake out a building with a high-power camera to take photos of badges and mock up fakes to use for gaining access.

I had been hoping to get a security badge for this company, as it was pretty tight from what little I could glean from descriptions; this was before Google street view, if you can imagine that.

I had a stroke of luck, as often comes with this type of work. Out of the blue, I heard that one of the sales guys in our company was going to visit the client to hash out some other work they wanted from us. I called the sales guy and persuaded him to help me infiltrate.

He found himself the willing bit-part in what must have felt to him like a spy novel. His mission was clear, I told him.

"Walk in and get your visitor badge, as normal. As soon as you can, excuse yourself to the bathroom, lock yourself in a cubicle, and place your badge on the white toilet seat". He was then to use the disposable camera he had on him (this was many years before the first camera phone became available) to take several shots of both sides of the badge, with and without flash. He would then get the film developed and send the photos to me to mock up the new badge.

Fast-forward several weeks later. I was ready to go into the building, do my assessment, and get done what the client needed.

I walked up to the office and through the first entranceway. On my right was a long, sleek reception desk with a fresh-faced, eager receptionist smiling at me. Her smile faded a little as it became clear I was walking straight to the security barriers and did not need her assistance.

As this was my first time in the building, I glanced around, taking stock of all the CCTV camera positions and any exits, entrances, and other places that might be of use later on. Something felt a little off, but I told myself it was probably just all new to me.

I noticed that the three security gates ahead were those terrible sliding glass pedestrian barriers. I would normally tailgate or jump them; however, to the right of the three normal barriers, there was a visitor barrier. This one was watched over by a security guard I wasn't told about by my stool pigeon. Damn it.

I pulled my fake badge out of my pocket and clipped it on my left hip, furthest from the security guard on my right, so he could not see it clearly. I walked up to the visitor barrier and flashed the badge with a weird hip twist. Expecting that to work, I stepped forward, but the barrier didn't open.

The security guard held up his hand and said, "Stop right there."

Internally, I panicked.

"Excuse me, sir, can I see that badge, please?"

Internally, I panicked some more.

"I am sorry, son, but I can't let you in with that badge."

More panic.

"Why not?" I managed to vocalize.

"It's wrong. It's out of date."

"What do you mean?" I asked, with questioning authority returning to my voice, "I have been using it for weeks to come and go. I'm working here temporarily."

"Not with that badge. We rebranded two weeks ago. That badge is the old one; you need to get it updated."

It was as he said those words that it dawned on me what was off. Everything—the name, the colors, the logos—had changed. The client had not told us this was due to happen. Here I was with an out-of-date, no-longer-used, branded fake badge, and there was that internal panic still raging.

Externally, however, I knew I couldn't skip a beat. Barely had my mind taken in this rather unfortunate news when I came up with a solution.

I grabbed my badge off my hip and slammed it down as hard as I could to make as much noise as possible and create a diversionary psychological trigger called an *interrupt*. Done correctly, interrupts can work wonders on people. As I slammed the badge down, I locked eyes with the receptionist, who had taken more interest in me since I was prevented from entering and had sidled down the desk toward us. I engaged her gaze, and without breaking it, I pointed at the security guard and said:

"You heard him. He needs you to update my pass straight away."

I emphasized the words so she understood that the decision and order came from the security guard and not from me.

She immediately processed me a new pass—no checks, no anything. I was issued a brand-new, real pass within a minute, and I turned to the security guard and said, "Is that better now?" in a slightly indignant tone.

The security guard nodded, and with my new card, I was about to walk through the visitor barrier when he stopped me again.

"You can use the normal barriers with that card."

I had been given a working card that gave me access to many places. Not only an *updated* pass but an *upgraded* pass.

The swan effect pays off: you may be panicking internally, but keep it calm on the surface.

Chapter 32

What's in the Box?

O ne of the key things you must do when performing this type of work is blend in. I have heard countless stories of people wearing Hi-Viz jackets or carrying a ladder or pretending to be pizza delivery. While that may work for them and whatever odd construction site, high school party, or light fixture shop they are trying to break into, normally a high-end bank won't let you in, no matter what. As mentioned before, reconnaissance is also vital for the success of any assessment. I will often spend three to four times longer watching and taking notes than I will perform-ing the job. I do use props, but often something like a hand-stitched Italian suit or a high-end Breitling watch, without which you would be spotted as an imposter in seconds by the people you are trying to infiltrate. Conversely, over-dressing for a small regional govern-ment office will also attract the wrong attention.

Physical props are annoying; they can be a beacon and remove your anonymity. You are supposed to be the "grey man," not stand out, not be identifiable, and certainly not be weighed down by props. But here is a story of one time I did use a prop.

The job I had to do was with a major HQ of a large high-street bank branch. It was relatively easy, and I completed my main task within an hour. During the washup meeting with the client, they were very impressed and asked if I minded trying to gain access again via a different entrance point (originally I came in via the main entrance). As I had many hours left on their clock, I agreed— and within a few hours, I was back in another washup meeting and considering what to do about lunch.

I was given a further offer: a luxury late lunch if I was able to gain access a third time. But this time I had to test a specific entrance, and the client chose to add an additional item: I had to interact with the reception staff to check their training. Now, normally I avoid talking to people when possible, but the offer of a nice lunch and the fact that I had already gained entry meant I had nothing to lose.

I made my way to a large loading bay that snaked down underneath the building. My goal here was not to gain entry—that would have been easy—but to get a useful prop.

This is a good time to point out the power of the right clothing. I was wearing a suit and in an area where people didn't wear suits. In the world of business, it often goes that those in suits have more important roles than those not in suits, so everyone in the loading bay just assumed I was supposed to be there. I walked around peeking into boxes and opening carts until I found what I needed: a large empty box.

I went into the rear entrance that was only used by staff and walked straight past the counter of the reception staff that I needed to test. I hefted the box up awkwardly and tried to swipe my non-existent ID badge against the reader. Obviously, this did not work. I made a bit of a scene and got the attention of the reception staff.

I carried the box over to the desk and, with faked effort, placed it on the desk; then I asked a reception staff person if she could give me a hand. She was unable to see me. I had intended this to help hide myself from detection. With zero effort, she moved the box to the side about a foot—fortunately, she never realized that I had been pretending it was super-heavy and she had apparently gained super strength!

After a short conversation as to who I was going to see and why the item hadn't gone in via the loading bay, she allowed me to pick up the box and then remotely opened the gate as I walked in. I had successfully infiltrated the building again, but this time using just an empty box. Thankfully, the super-strong receptionist never once considered me to be an attacker.

Chapter 33

How to Bypass an Elevator Security System

I have climbed in and out of a number of elevators in my life. Climbing down or up elevator shafts is incredibly dangerous and not for the faint-hearted; however, there is another way to move around when the elevator is locked down.

This technique will allow you to bypass almost any "inside the elevator" security system. For those of you who have never worked in a large corporate office building like those in New York or London, it might be hard to picture what I am describing.

Some elevators in hotels use this kind of system, too. You might just not have noticed it.

You enter an elevator, and you try to press a button to go to floor 7 or 31, for example. Only the elevator will not move unless you first swipe the appropriate key card against the reader. Some systems allow access to all floors, or they might only allow you to access certain floors. That depends on the building and its setup.

What do you do if you do not have the right key card? Be patient. Being patient in life can give you some incredible rewards. However, as with anything in life, you can often help the outcome by stacking the odds in your favor to move things along a little.

So here is how the attack works. Let's say, for example, that we wish to go from the ground floor to our target floor: the 4th floor. Maybe it's a shared building, and floors 3 and 4 are our target company but 1 and 2 are not in scope for us, because they are used by an entirely different company.

First, as always, do your recon work and then pick your time. Lunchtime is best for this, as people will be leaving the office regularly. You step into the elevator and stand at the back. Press nothing, and do nothing; just stand there. What will happen quickly if you pick the optimal time is that someone on one of the floors above will call the elevator. How else are they going to get out for their lunch?

The elevator rises to their floor. If you are unlucky, they will be from the floor 2 or 3. Do not react; just ride the lift back down with them. It's unlikely they noticed that you came up, not down, and even if they did, it's very unlikely they will say anything. Do not worry about staying in the lift when they leave, or if other people get in on the ground floor. Just stand in silence. This will work out! People are usually too busy thinking about themselves to pay much attention to those around them.

At some point, someone on the fourth floor will need to go to lunch and will call the elevator. Step out as if you are meant to be there, and voilà! You have now gained access to the target floor without ever using the key-card system. Congratulations: you are now an elevator hacker.

Chapter 34
The Loading Bay

The majority of companies focus all their security on the most obvious areas they think should be protected. I can promise that most security budgets go toward the main entrance of a company's site: 90% of the clients I interact with have very strong defenses on the outside and somewhere between OK and none on the inside. Multibillion-dollar companies are the same; in fact, the more money a company has, the less security is generally found inside.

The trouble is, there are many ways to enter a site or building. Security is like an onion: it consists of many layers, and each layer offers different protections. You cannot rely on a single security control, because it is likely that at some point one or more security controls will be breached or bypassed. Then the other layers must be able to resist the attack. You wouldn't jump out of an airplane with only one parachute—you always have a reserve, just like security!

Even when clients have put in some effort before I'm involved, it is clear there is still a misunderstanding about security. I've frequently gained access to a "secure" site by not using the front door.

Whenever I look at a building for the first time, I think about its use and who is going in and out daily. Whether using a digital system or a physical one, we could theoretically create a perfectly secure version of the building; the downside is that it would be unusable. These buildings (and their security systems) are designed to be used, but this use cannot always be predicted, so flaws seep into the design.

Most offices over a certain size have a loading bay. It may be as simple as a large set of doors to the rear or side; in other cases, it's a huge underground garage that fits 20 or more full-sized lorries and trailers. I once worked at a site with an entire train station in the loading bay under the building.

Because large vehicles have to enter and exit these areas, it's often much easier for an individual to sneak in here than through the main entrance. They could be under a vehicle, on top of it, or even walking beside it, all of which I have done myself. Several anecdotes in this book describe ways I have gained access to areas like these. It's one of my most-used entrances to get into a building.

The average security outlook seems to be able to deal with only a single magnitude of threat. Does the entrance fit a person? Let's worry only about people. Does the entrance fit a truck or car? Let's focus on stopping those. Very rarely do I encounter a system that works on multiple scales.

Additionally, strangers are often present in loading bays: daily visitors from delivery firms, drivers, couriers, builders and fitters, and even catering staff. This makes it easier to blend in as someone who belongs. But as I have mentioned elsewhere in this book, clothing matters. Wearing a builder's outfit onto the floor of a trading bank where expensive hand-finished suits, £3000 watches, and silk ties reign supreme will get you kicked out sharpish. Wearing a hand-finished suit, £3000 watch, and silk tie into a loading bay will cause everyone to think that management is there, and they will avoid you like the plague! I have never needed to wear a high-viz jacket to perform my assessments, although I hear that others find it very effective due to the consensus that wearing one makes you somehow unquestionably present.

I recall once being asked to test a new huge upgrade to an investment bank in London. Millions of pounds were spent on some of the most impressive systems I have seen a bank put in place. I walked into that bank with no drama whatsoever because literally zero had been spent on upgrading the loading bay security. I mean it; I saw the budget breakdowns, and not a single penny was spent on it.

I also subverted the security of a government building in Europe due to failure to protect a loading bay adequately. Ten years later, that report is still making waves in that building; I know because I bumped into someone at an event who was shocked to meet me there. It's nice to know my work has a lasting impact on people!

Chapter 35

The Escort

I t's weird how security works. With the right badge, the right attitude, and the right words, you can convince a professional to go against all of their training and instincts.

This is the crux of my work: convincing someone to do something they shouldn't.

In this case, the thing they shouldn't have done was let me in somewhere secure. I had gained access to my client's site via some of the other means already outlined in this book—it's scary how easily and often these techniques work. At some point toward the end of the day, I located the server room that housed the most valuable computer assets and was the target of my assessment.

Sometimes, when only a few people have access to a restricted area and those people rarely visit it, the challenge becomes a waiting game. If the entrance is well protected, you can't always break in. The only way into these places is to gain legitimate access.

I was able to track down a security person relatively easily, given the type of facility I was in. It also wasn't hard to convince them that I needed to speak to the main person in charge. I was shown into a cramped office where a heavyset, bearded gentleman sat. (If you know who Pearl is in the movie *Blade,* that will give you an idea of the scene.)

It was pretty clear that this person felt he was above everyone else. The best way to manipulate someone like that is with extreme flattery—make them feel as though they know better than you.

What transpired was a conversation with this chap that led him to believe I was sent from higher up to perform an interview about his work because he had been nominated for an award (with a cash prize!). The interview would be published on the internal corporate site, and maybe we could convince a local newspaper to run a small story about him.

He was very proud of his work and the security measures he had brought into the company. (Try not to laugh just yet!)

His greatest achievement was his years of work in protecting the company's data, with not a single recorded breach. He said, "We are like Fort Knox, but better." I grinned in agreement and demanded to know more.

About 20 minutes into my arduous task of listening to this chap, I pretended to be incredulous about his achievements. How could he protect a server room and never have any breaches? Surely the task was impossible even for this god-like security guru.

I was sworn to secrecy, but he was willing to show off the security of the server room!

What happened next will forever baffle me: he summoned the energy to stand up and stuff another donut into his mouth (his third jam donut in 30 minutes), grabbed his keys, and bade me follow him. I wondered how he would manage without his diet regime of a donut every 10 minutes.

I followed him as he gesticulated and talked down about the staff and the problems they gave him. We arrived at the server room, and CCTV cameras watched and recorded as the gentleman swiped his keycard and used a second set of keys to open the door. He failed to point out that the keys were not decent security keys, the CCTV was poor quality, and the keycard was a very easy-to-copy MIFARE type.

I let him talk inanely about the high-tech security systems that he had personally installed. Then, after a few minutes, I asked if I could take a couple of cool technology-filled photos for the article. He agreed, as long as I didn't get the security in the shot!

I walked around the square room, taking photos, while he stood near the door. I backed toward the door and motioned to him to make room. As he stepped back, I let the door slam shut behind me. I saw him strain for two seconds to look through the window and then give up.

He had to reswipe his keycard to reopen the door. The door was shut for less than 30 seconds, but in that short time, I placed stickers (replacements for USB sticks) on several key components. This was the simulated attack and proof that I had been left unattended.

I took a few more photographs as proof and wrapped up our interview.

The security guy was oblivious to what had just happened and didn't even scold me for letting the door shut. Maybe he was too sure of his security!

I wrote up my experience in a full report to the client, outlining everything described here and much more about the security failures perpetuated by this man. I do not like to single out people in reports unless that person's behaviour has a detrimental effect on the company; after all, that is what I am there to protect.

The main issue I reported was not that I was escorted to and left alone in a server room for 30 seconds. Believe me, I can do a lot of damage in that time—but the company's security was compromised by the attitude and "iron fist" of this head of department. I have no idea what happened to him; I never recommend firing someone, and I advocate that decent and up-to-date training be provided to all individuals.

I did make recommendations to update the security mechanisms in place. I also recommended that in the future, people not ever be escorted to the most valuable data.

Chapter 36

The Staircase

Doing the walkaround with the head of security after one test, I mentioned that I would next show him the underground parking tunnel. He looked at me, genuinely puzzled, and said, "But we don't have underground parking." I knew that the next 10 minutes were going to be pretty fun.

The building was only two floors high and nestled between other buildings in a large business complex. I led him up to the CEO's office. We said hello to the personal assistant (PA), who was sitting at her desk, guarding the three directors' offices behind her. We passed her desk and veered into a small alcove to the left. I headed toward a thin, short door that looked more like a cleaner's cupboard. It was situated so that someone could walk from the directors' offices to the door without the PA seeing. I opened the small cupboard door and disappeared in.

I can only imagine what the security head was thinking when he saw me step into the cupboard and vanish like Lucy stepping into Narnia. Eventually, he worked up the courage to stick his head over the threshold, and his eyes popped. I stood several feet below him, perched on the bottom of a large spiral staircase.

I beckoned to him to come down the stairs, and we passed through another small door similar to the one we had entered. On the other side was a tiny underground garage that held only three cars.

Most people become accustomed to their surroundings. They don't challenge what's around them or the version of reality they are presented with. So, countless people likely walked past that door and, without even engaging their conscious brain, assumed it was a cupboard containing mops, a vacuum, bleach, and rubber gloves. But because as I take an attacker's view on life, I like to look in cupboards. You never know where Narnia might be, and instead of lions and witches, you may find shiny BMWs and Ferraris!

The head of security had never been told that below his building was an access point. Granted, he had not been in his role very long, and maybe people forgot to mention it or it wasn't documented for security reasons. The point is that even when you believe you know every single security point in your building, you cannot trust what you have not verified yourself.

This was a fun assessment with a lovely surprise, but the overall takeaway is to ensure that you inspect everything everywhere. Life has a way of being more exciting when you are willing to open doors for yourself.

Chapter 37

How to Bypass PIR Detectors

Passive infrared (PIR) detectors are among the most ubiquitous security mechanisms after keys and locks. Most people have interacted with one, even though you may not know what one is.

These detectors sense the presence of a person near a door. So, every time you walk into a store with automatic sliding doors, you are picked up by a PIR detector. Outside lights that come on when you walk into the garden, driveway, or parking lot are also PIR detectors. They are used for convenience in many areas of our lives and for alarm systems and security where detecting a person or movement can alert a guard or call for the police.

PIR detectors come in many forms, but they all work similarly. Essentially, they see infrared light, which equates somewhat to heat. Inside the detector are two or more pyroelectric sensors that sit beside each other. A pyroelectric sensor generates electricity when heated or cooled. Placing two of these sensors side by side and then comparing the two electric signals can determine if one is hotter than the other. If there is a big difference, the sensor sounds the alarm.

If a person enters the room, one sensor will pick up the additional heat in the room, thus creating a difference between the two pyroelectric sensors, and the alarm will sound.

The face of a PIR always has a lens (which often appears opaque white) that allows infrared light through. Each lens is faceted, meaning it's segmented. This creates a series of zones. Each zone is at a different angle in the room.

Here is a photo of a PIR detector; you can make out the facets on the lens.

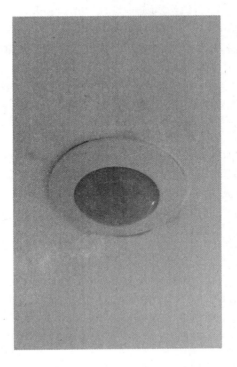

The lens intensifies the IR light hitting the sensor, which means differences are much easier to detect between zones. A person standing in the middle of a zone now generates a bigger signal than one at the edge of a zone—but how does that help? If a person moves between zones, say by walking across a room, they constantly break different zones, and the signal generated by the pyroelectric sensor rises and falls very quickly. This can only happen if a person moves across the zones, so the alarm will sound.

Once we know how these detectors work, we can reverse-engineer methods to circumvent them.

We know the sensor relies on temperature, so one way is to heat the entire room. However, for this to work, you would need to heat the whole room to the same temperature as a human body—the sensors wouldn't be able to differentiate between a person and a desk or a chair if everything was hot! This is impractical in almost every circumstance.

You could go the other way and cool yourself down to the same temperature as the room. But that is also impractical as you would probably die or not be functioning very well. You could wear a fancy IR-blocking suit and helmet, but you would be noticed if you were walking around looking like a knight dressed in aluminium foil.

Those methods would attack the sensors' ability to compare the background temperature, but there are easier ways.

Most alarm systems focus on the timing between zones. This avoids the alarm being triggered by, say, a computer left on a desk that powers up overnight and slowly warms up several zones, or a radiator. Remember, the detector is looking for quick pulses from several zones being heated in succession.

Walking very, very slowly across a room prevents this pulsing and stops the alarm from being triggered. You can try this at home to prove it works. If you have an outside detector light, it's a great party game to play with friends in the evening. Place an item near the light, and get people to walk as slowly as possible to pick it up!

You will be amazed by how quickly you can walk and not set it off, and you should observe a few other issues when playing. The most impactful in this case is that your orientation to the zones matters. Walking toward the sensor rather than perpendicular to the sensor makes it much harder to detect you, as you may stay in a single zone. Walking across forces you to move between zones. Try it, and see if you can catch your friends out!

Most commercial or consumer detectors also have a red light that shows the detector is working even when the alarm system is deactivated. You can practice on the ones in your office—a fun game if you are bored at work!

The simplest method I've used is a pane of glass. IR does not pass through glass easily and, in most cases, is blocked entirely. During an assessment, I broke into a specialist building. The room I was asked to gain access to had some interesting items in a small inner office space where there was monitoring equipment. This room had a door into the main space—and that main space was protected by a PIR system to the right of the door. I had to block it, or I would have set it off due to its superb placement.

I removed the window from the monitoring office; it was in a slide system, like you see at a doctor's office, so no damage was done.

I opened the door and very slowly lifted the pane of glass into the view of the PIR detector. Using the wall and the ceiling tiles, I wedged the pane of glass so it sat between the detector and the room. Because the glass was already at the ambient room temperature, and because I moved slowly to block it, the detector was now unable to "see" through the glass, and I could move around the room at normal speed and perform the actions I needed to.

I replaced the glass pane without any issues and left.

I hope you can see that with a good understanding of how a security mechanism or detector works, you can easily reverse-engineer methods to attack or circumvent it. I would be remiss if I did not mention that some of these techniques can be seen in the amazing Robert Redford movie *Sneakers*; if you haven't already, you should watch it. The characters perform a job similar to mine, and it's nice to see them doing it correctly.

Chapter 38

ATMs

It is often said that when Willie Sutton, the famous bank robber, was asked why he robbed banks, he replied, "It's where the money is." Unfortunately, he never said that, but there is some truth to it.

ATMs hold a lot of money. They are also just computers in big metal boxes. These two facts make them fantastic targets for attackers.

Willie Sutton also said that he used a machine gun because "You can't rob a bank on charm and personality." I am living proof that Sutton was very wrong on this point.

In the 1995 cult movie classic *Hackers*, an attack against an ATM caused money to be given out. Skip forward to 2010, when the renowned hacker Barnaby Jack (1977–2013) gave a live demonstration of a similar attack at the BlackHat hacker conference.

These attacks relied on sophisticated techniques. Jack and his teammates worked incredibly hard to attack an ATM from the street side. But there is a much, much easier way to achieve this.

Most ATMs run a version of Windows on a PC hidden inside. But how do you get to it? Barnaby Jack figured out one way, but as with almost every "secure" device, there is always another way in. The bank has to do two things with an ATM: allow the tellers to refill the money (and remove it if the ATM takes deposits) and allow maintenance staff to perform their duties. Both of these tasks occur inside the bank, generally when it is closed to the public. So how can you attack the ATM?

I had been tasked with gaining access to several bank machines across the UK. The idea was to gain access to the computers behind the desks used by the bank tellers. The task was insane: somehow, I had to walk in off the street and convince staff to let me into the bulletproof and highly secured teller area and then allow me to either take over the computer or gain physical access to the machine to implant hardware that would give me remote control.

Surprisingly, this was much easier than everyone (including me!) expected. Over several days, I gained access to more than a dozen computers being used by tellers to perform bank transfers, withdrawals, deposits, foreign exchange (forex), and much more. I had physical access and administrative access to all of them. Each day I used the same trick, so on the last day, I assumed I would do so again. I walked into the lobby area and saw, to my astonishment, an ATM wide open and being worked on by a repairman. I watched as he and the manager walked away to an office, leaving the poor, defenceless ATM exposed to the world.

Being open to taking any opportunity that presents itself, I decided the machine required further inspection. I loitered near it, peering in and then eventually braving a few snaps. After a few minutes, I realized that no one was watching me. I edged closer and closer and finally gave in.

I reached into the ATM and pulled on the draw that held the PC. The drawer came back and out toward me, and I leaned down and implanted my device directly into the ATM. I was sure someone would appear at this stage.

Dear reader, they did not.

I carefully replaced the draw and hung around. After all, I didn't want a real criminal to have access to the ATM—I was there to prevent a crime, not enable it.

The client was as excited as I was that I had managed to gain access that way. It's refreshing when a client responds like this, as it shows they have a good understanding of security.

Policies and procedures were changed at over 100 branches because of my actions. The bank's policies about how and when repairs are carried out are still in place today. It is safer for a bank to carry out these types of activities with the bank shut up and whilst I understand the frustration of a bank closing during the day, I assure you that the alternative is much worse for everyone.

By the way, you might think it is rare for an ATM to be left unguarded. But a few weeks ago I was with my wife in a strange town, and while in a bank, I noticed that the street-facing ATM was similarly open and abandoned. I took a photo to share with you. (I again waited to ensure that the ATM was safe until the repair chap reappeared.)

Chapter 39

Open Windows

It boggles my mind that people rely more on locks than any other security measure. I have said for decades, and still do, that locks only keep honest people out. Locks are there to keep out the opportunistic and those who don't break the law. A lock, as you have seen and learned, can be bypassed with ease. The trouble is, criminals go for the even easier route.

How many burglaries have you read about that involved a criminal picking the lock or replicating a key, versus how many kicked the door in or smashed a window?

People are sold on a £100 deadbolt lock but fail to see that the hollow wood door and even weaker door frame are not up to the task.

When I am asked to perform security assessments, it is my job to point out every issue I can, including things like door frames. But now and then, I see security issues that even a non-security person should be able to pick up on.

In three cases, I have been tasked with breaking into sites at night. These sites were protected by all sorts of controls, from night vision CCTV to barbed wire fencing, high-security lock systems, roaming guards, and fancy alarm systems. And yet in every case, I found a ground-level window wide open.

It takes zero skill to climb through a window. You don't have to silently break it, and you don't have to worry about window sensors or move latches to help your entry. Just swing the window wide open and climb in like a common cat burglar in a movie.

I cannot count how many targets I have compromised by utilizing windows. One anecdote worth mentioning is the time I was asked to verify the security of a building containing precious gems. No, not the one I mentioned in Chapter 24, "What Do I Know about Diamonds?", or the one I got locked into. This was a low-level, single-story building housing millions of precious gems that were being graded and sorted. You can probably picture the scene from a dozen movies: old men with tweezers and magnifying glasses hunched over brightly lit tables.

The small, squat building blended into the background of its surroundings with surprising ease; I could have walked past the building a thousand times and never gotten a hint of what was inside. The loading area at the back was well-protected, and the front door was heavy and protected but blended in nicely. Small windows around head height peppered the outside, and grates protected them.

As I was performing my walkaround, trying to match the foot traffic, I was almost smacked in the head as someone inside swung a window open! Not one to wait around when given such fantastic luck, I grabbed a bunch of blu-tack (an adhesive putty) from my bag, rolled it into a large ball, and stuck it into the window frame.

The night of my assessment, I walked up to the now-shut window—and saw that my plan had succeeded. The blu-tack had made it very difficult to shut the window fully. A small gap had been left where the window bent slightly around the blu-tack. It didn't take long to remove the metal grate screwed to the wall. A bit of swift jimmying with a screwdriver got the window open, and all I had to do was climb through it!

I found that the easiest way in was to climb onto the roof and lower myself feet first through the window. When I was about half-way in, a group of local youths wandered past and asked what I was doing. It's hard to explain my job at the best of times, and I was not sure these teens would be able to grasp the enormity of the contents of the building or that I was not breaking the law. So I told them there was a fiver for each of them if they could get me a ladder and be back in 10 minutes.

Now, I would be lying to you if I said that breaking into a place like this is glamorous. It's not. What happened next as I slid into the room was that the upper half of my clothing got caught on a latch, dragging it up and over my head and rendering me blind as well as unable to use my hands. I felt my foot land on something, and as I put my weight on it, I slipped and landed squarely in the toilet bowl. The next few minutes saw me re-dressing and squelching as I moved around the rooms leaving stickers and removing a couple of valuable items.

Ten minutes later, I pulled myself out of the window was surprised to see a small ladder. A very helpful group of teens made a small bit of cash for helping me take around £600,000 in gems.

Needless to say, my recommendations to the client to move their facility to a much more secure location were taken up at breathtaking speed. They had relied on security by obscurity and not much else. The new facility has an incredible display of security and would be a challenge to me if I hadn't helped design it.

Chapter 40

Security on a String Budget

Security budgets are always tight, and each year it seems harder to convince companies to spend money on something that does not bring in profit. It is difficult to measure the success of security because you do not see the attacks that don't or can't happen.

When it comes to governments, they have even tighter budgets. Because of this, some of their sites can—well, let me be kind here: they can be of poor quality when it comes to security.

I have been lucky enough to work with many government agencies as part of my career. So, I have seen and fought against the red tape that can keep even the simplest security issue from being fixed. Some of my findings when working with governments around the world can be rather shocking to members of the public, who only find out about them after they have been fixed.

A government department (I can't say which) once asked me to perform an assessment of a site. It was a small, squat building, only two stories, with a single-story flat-roofed extension to the side. The site was not particularly interesting. It did not have any perimeter protection, as it was in the middle of a city and surrounded by other dull buildings. It always looked to me like a downtrodden library on the brink of closure, but inside were some very interesting technologies that I am certainly not allowed to talk about.

Gaining access into the building for my assessment was very easy, not just because I am experienced at it, but because it literally had holes in its security. However, things got much more interesting after I had finished my task. As always at the end of an assessment,

I took the client around the site and pointed out the issues I noted. When we went up to the second floor—the part that overlooked the flat roof—there in front of us was a large metal-framed window. The window latch was closed, but no window locks were visible. The government employees had cleverly wound string around the latch to prevent the window from being opened.

To me, the most horrific thing was not that this was a government site and the entrance was being secured by a piece of string, nor that it was in a run-down building that could barely keep out the cold British wind, let alone a determined attacker. The worst thing was that this wasn't the only time I have seen string used to "lock" a door, window, or other supposedly secure location.

Throughout my career, I have seen many buildings secured in weird ways—but buildings are not the only thing secured by inappropriate means.

Computers are also often left insecure. I don't mean digitally secure, and I am not talking about the desktop or laptop you work with. I mean the servers that run all the important stuff: the big, beefy computers that sit in wardrobe-sized racks in even larger warehouses. They run the telephone systems, your office intranet, your email, and your SharePoint system and contain tons of data—including customer data and financial data.

My job covers hacking into computer systems like this—and believe me, it's pretty easy most of the time—but this book is more about the physical security side of things, and that's what I mean here. In my experience, computer servers are rarely physically secured, despite their value to the company.

For instance, take this server rack.

This rack of computers was not in a fancy data center; it was what we refer to as "on-prem" or on-premises. That means it was in a normal office building. The first mistake was that it was not in a locked room but rather was on the office floor as though it was nothing more than a printer. Anyone who could get on the floor could walk over to it.

The cabinet had a door, at least, but the lock was broken. The poor cable management at the front prevented the door from being kept shut, so the staff's ingenious solution was to tape the door closed.

Any malicious person or someone thinking they were being funny could have pulled out a cable (even the power cables) and completely ruined this company's infrastructure, possibly catastrophically.

If any reader still needs to hear this, tape, string, or anything similar is not a secure locking mechanism. That said, even secure locking mechanisms have vulnerabilities. In the next chapter, we will talk about locks—in particular, padlocks—and how to pick and bypass them. I will also show you why I am always saying "Locks only keep honest people out."

Chapter 41

How to Bypass Padlocks

P adlocks: what can I say about them? They are basically useless as a security mechanism. As I have said many times in life and this book, locks only keep honest people out. And with padlocks, we see the same thing.

Padlocks come in all shapes, sizes, and qualities and share the same flaws.

Like all security mechanisms, they are designed to slow attackers down, not stop them entirely. But when they are installed incorrectly, or the wrong type is used, it's often quicker to bypass the lock than use the correct key. Padlocks are funny because they are not the physical thing that prevents a door or gate from opening—although they might seem like it. The physical barrier is what the padlock attaches to: inevitably, a hole or loop on the door/gate and another on the framework.

I have seen expensive padlocks attached to wooden frames that are falling apart; a swift tug will pull the screws out of the framework. People often forget that criminals can use screwdrivers and unscrew most attachments, so these must also be protected.

The elephant in the room or padlock that I will not discuss in this chapter is the keyway itself. The lock and key portion is almost always susceptible to lock picking, and I cover how to pick a lock in Chapter 54. This chapter is about how to circumvent padlocks without a key.

Padlocks are one of the easiest-to-attack security mechanisms because they are often cheap, left alone, and exposed. While I do my best in my job not to damage anything, padlocks are usually inexpensive and easy to replace. It's also often in the client's best interests to *not* use a padlock and instead replace it with something better.

Here are some ways you can destroy a padlock to gain entry:

- *Heat:* Melt it. Many padlocks are alloys with low melting points and can easily be melted. Over a decade ago, I helped a friend, Steve 'autom8on' Wilson, design a pocket-sized portable thermal lance. Almost nothing can stop a thermal lance (a large stick of iron that is burned in oxygen and produces temperatures over 4,000 degrees Fahrenheit). It will burn through anything to a depth of around 18 inches—hardened steel and concrete melt. A padlock will melt like butter even using a normal blowtorch.
- *Cold:* Any metal becomes incredibly brittle when cooled. Pouring liquid nitrogen over a padlock and hitting it hard with a large hammer will obliterate it. If I am honest, a blow to most padlocks with a hammer will smash it even without cooling it first.
- *Cutting:* Under a certain size, cutting a padlock is extremely easy. A pair of 12-inch bolt croppers will cut through most of them. Larger padlocks may require larger bolt cutters or a hydraulic cutter.
- *Force:* There are many ways to force open a padlock. A common technique is to insert the ends of two large open-end spanners into the gap and pry it open. (This is hard to describe in words, but many online videos show how incredibly easy it is.) Another method is to use a small bottle jack if there is room to force the lock off or open.

Most low-security locks have only one catch, which is held in place by a spring. Another fantastic method I have used is hitting the padlock—not hard enough to destroy it, but enough to use physics against the lock. If the spring sits left to right, pushing the catch to the right into the hasp (the round loop part of the padlock), hitting the padlock from the left will cause the padlock to move right. But inertia will make the spring compress, and the catch will stay stationary in space. As the position of the latch and the catch are now different, the hasp will open. It's tricky to get right, but when it works, it looks like magic. You can also use this technique on small personal safes.

- *Drilling:* Use a good drill to drill the keyway; it's slow but effective. With no keyway or pins, there is no lock. This works on most low- to medium-security padlocks.
- *Shimming:* This is my preferred method after picking. A shim is a thin piece of metal forced between the hasp and the body (the big part you stick the key into). Inside the body are one or two catches that align with notches in the hasp, and when it is closed, they are engaged. When the key is inserted and turned, the catches retract, and the hasp can open. Shimming essentially forces the catches back into the body. You can buy various types of shims cheap online, or you can make your own using a soda can. Again, I suggest watching videos online to see how to make and use them.

Chapter 42
Padlocked Gates

I hope you now appreciate how weak a padlock is and why it shouldn't be used to secure any area—at least, nothing serious, and never on its own.

In my career, I must have seen thousands of padlocks in silly places: doors, cupboards, and gates, all of which might as well not have a lock on them. It's not just padlocks, either; normal key locks (the type used on houses) are all insecure. You can get the lock-picks described in the previous chapter as well as specialist tools that can help you gain access to many locations. Most aren't even illegal (please check local laws).

The keys shown here are my personal set of what are known as *bump* keys. This small set of keys is precisely made to work on any door with a "yale" type of keyway. It is estimated that this small set would work for around 90% of buildings in the UK. Frightening, really, considering all the buildings, outhouses, sheds, garages, and homes that contain incredibly valuable things, while this set of keys costs less than £50 at the time of writing.

Unless you have the skills described in the previous chapter or some of the specialist tools—such as bump keys, comb picks, electric picks, pick guns, or even shims—you will be like 99% of the population that thinks a padlock or door lock is safe. The sad and honest truth is that you have been sold a lie.

"Locks only keep honest people out." I say this many times a month to clients and people who attend my talks.

But sometimes it is not the lock that is the problem. Security is rarely about the product or mechanism. It is often more important how and where it is used.

Let me give a nice example of how I think compared to the average person when it comes to securing something as simple as a large gate.

A client asked us to look at their facility. They knew they had to do some work on physical security but told us they had "expert" advice and felt pretty confident that their facility was as secure as possible.

I arrived mid-morning for a walkthrough of the facility, which held some valuable objects. The front was pretty well locked down, and side entrances, windows, etc., were all within good industry standards. I gave the client some general advice about minor improvements.

We walked around the back of the facility where most of the action happened. Trucks came into a gated area, unloaded or loaded, and left again. The loading bays were pretty insecure: it was possible to open them from the outside due to staff needing access 24/7. The client countered by saying that CCTV was watching 24/7, only five trucks (and their drivers) had access via a locked gate, and everything was logged in a book.

First, criminals never write their comings and goings in log books, which will never help anyone but an auditor.

Second, the 24/7 CCTV system was not watched by a security team. It was just recording. And if an incident happened, they had almost a week of old footage to trawl through.

Finally, we came to the gate. "Wow," I said when I saw it for the first time. The client thought I was impressed.

The gate was impressive to look at: it was bright blue, for one thing! The barrier crossed the gap in the wall, you couldn't walk around it, and it looked nice and thick.

But there were many things wrong with this gate. As I sit at my keyboard writing this paragraph, I am not sure where to start.

The gate was padlocked with possibly the cheapest padlock I have ever seen—looking at it the wrong way might have even broken it. The barrier hinged on flimsy posts, and the hinges themselves were the type that could be lifted off. So even if the lock gave you trouble, the gate could be easily lifted off its hinges and opened to that side (probably more quickly than using the key).

The final nail in the coffin was that they had installed this abomination of security on a brick wall about 4 feet high.

I ducked under the single barrier that formed the main protection and, without saying anything, jumped up and over the wall, walked across the yard, and opened the side door to the loading bay with a lock pick. Once inside, I opened the main door into the courtyard and walked back to the client.

At no point had they considered that a lone person would try to enter the premises; they only thought about trucks. After explaining all the flaws in their gate, locks, wall, and approach to security, we double-checked their CCTV system. Its main components were stuffed in a cupboard and attached to a pretty shoddy VHS tape recorder with no one watching it. We rewound the tape and caught approximately 7 seconds of me on low-definition, low-light, grainy, fuzzy film. I was barely able to recognize myself.

This site was basically being protected by two locks, both of poor quality and one installed in a way that made it easier to bypass than to use. I still think about that gate and who the "expert" was that they called in to help them secure their site.

Poor padlocks are used in a huge number of places, but to this day, when I see one, it still surprises me. I often come across as weirdly obsessed when I point this out in my day-to-day non-working life.

Here is a photograph of another poor padlock being used to secure a cage that held incredibly sensitive documents. For some reason, they felt that putting the cage in the basement of a building was sufficient to lower their inside security standards.

Chapter 43

The Security of Glass

This story takes place in a European bank that asked us to do some work as part of a larger piece of work. This, I think, highlights several facets of security.

I am never off duty when it comes to security. Walking around shopping malls, streets, on holiday, or even in my own village, I spot security issues everywhere, and sometimes I am in the fortunate position to tell people about them. I used to tell strangers about their security issues, but that caused them to be suspicious or made me look weird and paranoid.

In this instance, my wife and I were flown over and given the VIP treatment. On arrival, we were met by a car and taken to our plush hotel. The next morning, another car picked us up in the rain and took us to the client's incredible headquarters—a fabulous glass and steel monument to wealth.

We performed our tasks, and the client was incredibly happy with our work. At the end of the day, we were given a tour that ended at the non-official main entrance. The building was made of two separate buildings connected by a covered corridor, and I noticed we hadn't come in this way.

As we walked through the lobby, I saw this.

I was shocked. I pointed to the monstrous white man-trap in the middle of the lobby, bolted to the floor and standing eerily out of place like a monolith in the movie *2001: A Space Odyssey*.

You can probably see a few issues with it from a security point of view. My brain was having an aneurysm just looking at it.

Who in their right mind wouldn't just walk around this thing? No fencing, barrier, odd placement, ladder construction, cameras, guards, security bolts, or authentication mechanism—you could have easily bypassed, attacked, or stolen this gate! The fact that it had no mechanism to authenticate the crazy individual who would use it meant it simply revolved—how on earth was that supposed to be security?

I couldn't contain myself any longer than the three seconds required to take it all in.

"What the hell is that thing doing?" I asked, pointing at the monolithic waste of space.

"It's a security barrier . . ." The client's voice was already starting to waver, as they could sense this wasn't going to go well. They instantly tried to placate me.

"It's obviously not a permanent security barrier; we find it very effective, though."

"Against what? Floor cleaners?" I could barely restrain myself.

"Well, it's for random checks. On random days, we take that rope barrier and cordon off the area so everyone has to use the gate."

"?????"

"We then place a security guard on duty to enforce it, and they check everyone's badges as they pass through the gate."

"????"

"We pick the day completely at random, so no one knows, so a criminal couldn't possibly know if he was about to walk in and find all this security around."

I proceeded to point out that a single guard cannot both check IDs and maintain a large barrier. I also learned that "completely at random" wasn't true: they never used the gate two days in a row, or on holidays, or if anyone senior was coming in.

I decided to lay the bombshell that was about to obliterate any last hope for this poor door system.

"So, the random barrier thing will prevent criminals from attacking because they won't know if it's in place?"

"Correct."

"Say a criminal walked up the steps from the street. As they approached the door, where would they be looking?"

"Er . . . at the door? The front of the building?"

"Yes! Which is made from what?

"Er . . . glass?" The client was gaining clarity about the situation as the syllables fell from their mouth.

A criminal walking up to the front of the building could look through the massive glass windows and see the barrier system in place before they got within 20 feet of the door—allowing them to turn around and come back tomorrow.

Glass is one of the worst materials when it comes to security. Not only can you see through glass, but it's often easy to break, and you can even hear through it. Some sophisticated attacks have used lasers from a significant distance to pick up vibrations from glass and objects, such as crisp packets inside a room, and turn them back into audio.

When I was in previous roles, a lot of time was spent in secure windowless rooms or rooms-within-rooms known as SCIFs (sensitive compartmented information facilities). The reason for this type of layout is that it removes all the security issues that windows create.

Chapter 44

Trading Places

In society there are certain rules and ways of working that are not familiar to many of us. Most people start a new job and find it takes a while to settle in—the cliques from school, college, or even university are still a thing when you get into a workplace. You have in crowds, you have loners, you have the nerds, the sports buffs, the managers, the suck-ups, and the weirdos. Add office politics to that, and you might as well be back in high school!

The first few months in a workplace can seem strange as you're trying to navigate the unwritten rules of how to do your job. On top of that, there are the actual rules. Sometimes they can be weirder than the unwritten rules.

It's hard for many people to imagine how old some banks are in England. Some were established in the 1700s, and a few even earlier than that! Over 300 years of traditions are set in the normal rules of working as well as longstanding odd things: for example, I know of one bank with a rule that women *must* be shown through a door first and must even ride the elevator by themselves, lest they be left alone with a man. That bank also prohibits women on certain floors; men must come down to their floor (and it's always down!).

At another bank, ever since the popularity of bowler hats, their bankers have had to wear them *in* the office for specific events such as the opening and closing of the markets.

How people dress is a huge concern to me in my job. Unlike most people who perform social engineering, my role requires blending in with the staff. A high-viz jacket, ladder, and clipboard that might be perfect for a small office block or building site would never work in the environments I often break into—work like that would be done outside office hours. To give you an example, I once made the mistake of entering an investment bank wearing the wrong watch. By "wrong," I mean I walked in with a very nice, semi-expensive Casio watch. I was almost immediately spotted by two staff members and outed as not belonging to their department; within three minutes, I was nicknamed "Casio Boy." Joke's on them—a few weeks later I was able to enter their department, this time wearing a £3500 Breitling watch. I was ignored. They didn't even recognize my face; they just saw that the watch fit!

It's not only watches that you need to get right. Footwear can also give you away. Not to mention your suit. Every company has little pockets of "culture" that make up cliques. You might have come across some of them in your time. The drinking culture, the clubbing culture, the gaming culture, the cyclists, the fitness buffs, the watch one-uppers, everyone trying their best to outdo the others. Who has the most expensive bike? Who has the latest fad drink? Who has the best watch? Who stayed out latest and still made the meeting?

Suits are a huge source of competition. I really hate suits, so I never see the appeal. Once an assessment was delayed by over a month because the client told me everyone wore a handmade Italian suit. I had to go online and order one made, but thankfully the cost was passed to the client.

I once broke into a very large investment bank, but not the type you see on the high street—think more of the Wall Street type of bank with stockbrokers and people shouting over phones. My job that day was to see if I could place stickers (representatives of USB sticks containing nefarious things) on computers throughout the building. It had been heavily suggested that I would be caught straight away.

As I walked onto the trading floor, I assumed it would be like most I had visited—warm!

I found myself in a small hall outside the trading office, and in preparation, I slipped off my tie and folded it into my pocket. I unbuttoned my shirt collar but kept my jacket on, as I had a kit in it that I needed.

I took a deep breath and walked in like I owned the place.

"What the f*** are you doing, you twat!" someone almost immediately yelled at me. Wow, what a welcome!

He was sitting at a desk with a phone cradled on one shoulder and another in his left hand. He motioned to me to come over to him.

"You want to get me fired, you *****?" I stared blankly, unsure of what I had done to bring down such vitriol from this stranger.

He pulled open a desk drawer, and it contained about a dozen rolled-up silk ties with various garish designs. He picked a purple and yellow paisley-patterned tie and threw it at me.

"Put that on quick, you t*****, before Mike sees you!"

In this room, the rule was "no tie, no trade." Apparently, despite the heat and toxic masculinity of the room, everyone had to wear a tie all the time. This was before video calls, so I have no idea who the hell they were trying to impress. But hey, I got a free silk tie out of it, so who am I to complain?

This wasn't the only wardrobe error I've made, either.

I spent weeks watching a bank headquarters, taking note of the dress code before eventually picking my day. I walked into the reception area, avoided the reception staff, and hid out of sight of the lone security guard. I sat on a small bench, waiting for a chance to slip past unnoticed.

It was as I was assessing the situation that I noticed the dinosaur.

A young chap walked across from the main door to the security barrier in a bright green-and-yellow dinosaur onesie with a tail and spikes. Not your normal outfit to wear to work in a bank.

I then began looking at the other people around me. Various accouterments adorned their bodies: the receptionist wore cat's ears and had whiskers drawn on her face, and the security guard was holding a little devil's pitchfork.

Just then, Jack Sparrow, Wolverine, and James bond walked in.

I decided to leave. It was clear by this point that a man in a cheap suit would not blend in with a charity costume event!

Chapter 45

How to Bypass Keypads

I thought I'd include a quick chapter on bypassing keypads. I see these almost daily, and there is never a job that happens without me finding one that is being used to secure a door.

Like all security mechanisms, keypads vary from really nice to "OMG, I can't believe you bought that." They also range from purely mechanical to sophisticated electronics. But it often comes down to how they are installed more than the device itself. Keypads can offer some protection against attacks but are frequently installed poorly, are of cheap quality, or are easy to bypass.

Before we get too far, I want to share a photograph of a poor example of a keypad.

Here, as you can see, the whole thing has been subverted by someone writing the code on the wall.

These types of mechanical pads can be bypassed most of the time using a rare-earth magnet run along the side. In fact, many locks can be bypassed using strong magnets. But keypads of all types have another, more intrinsic flaw: brute forcing.

My local gym, for example, has keypads on the lockers. They are a mix of digital and mechanical buttons, but they all use the same type of code. Press the clear button, enter four digits, and then press the Lock button. To unlock the locker, press the clear button, enter the same four digits, and then press Unlock.

Four digits. That's all. Keypad systems rarely use more than six 6 digits. Guessing numbers and trying to unlock a keypad is called *brute forcing;* although the name and method seem like a low-IQ attempt to circumvent security, it's often very effective.

The same type of attack can be used on anything that uses four-, six-, or even eight-digit combinations: bike locks, gym lockers, safes, PINs for credit cards, and security doors to access top-secret information.

You can start with 0000 and then progress through 0001, 0002, 0003 . . . to 9999. That will guarantee you get in because you will try every combination available—what we call the number of *permutations.* It takes a long time, but you will for sure get in. You can cheat a bit and try common number combinations first: 1234, for example.

Most sophisticated systems avert this type of attack by preventing more than three or four guesses or not allowing another guess until a certain number of seconds has passed. This doesn't prevent the attack but can slow it immensely. However, attackers can play the long game and try over several days or even months if the combination does not change often.

This lockout-prevention approach is never used on purely mechanical systems—to be honest, some low-end electronic systems don't use it either. My gym doesn't have a lockout-prevention mechanism (by the time you read this, I will have moved from this gym, which is why I don't mind telling you).

If the lock you are attacking is in a position where you cannot spend the time to brute force or make educated guesses, there are other attacks.

You can use a thermal imagining camera; even a cheap one you attach to a phone will work. The latent heat left behind after someone uses the correct code can help you narrow down the keys tremendously.

Another technique is to cover the keypad in UV-reactive ink. It's invisible to the naked eye but is rubbed off certain keys when they're used and can then be seen with a UV light. You can even reverse this and get the ink onto the target's hand, but doing so is much harder.

There are many variations of this approach, from waxes to inks, but they all rely on the same premise.

You can always shoulder surf, a technique where you position yourself or a camera to observe the keypad when someone uses it, noting the code and reusing it later. Shields and education can make this hard work in some places.

Electronic keypads can be very sophisticated—some have touchscreens that display buttons, and the positions of the numbers change with every use. I have seen this become more common over the last few years. These types of keypads can be tricky to bypass using the methods I have described.

Another way to attack a keypad system is to open it. I have yet to see a keypad with a built-in tamper alarm. However, I need to offer a caveat about this attack: it only works on self-contained keypad systems, i.e., where the "intelligence" portion is in the keypad itself.

Opening a keypad reveals a small computer system; the entire code-checking system is self-contained. The key code is input by the target using the key buttons, and the computer confirms the valid code and sends a small electrical signal to the door-locking mechanism (often a maglock, as discussed in Chapter 61). This signal is normally a continuous 5 volt charge. If you are lucky enough to have a self-contained keypad like this, a small short across the contacts will often pop the door open. Not every keypad is susceptible to this attack, but I have used it many times. The layouts may differ, but the way it works is the same.

If you have a keypad system more sophisticated than this and you are a beginner, I suggest that you look for other entry methods. Often there is more than one way to bypass a system.

Chapter 46

E-Waste

Recycling is great; it's environmentally friendly and saves vast amounts of energy. What it doesn't do, though, is help with security.

I remember being asked to break into a commercial office space. It was the headquarters of a tech company, and by this point in the book you are probably well aware of how it went. I highlighted several security issues, and the company did a wonderful job of fixing them.

Months later, I returned to the office and had a fantastic washup meeting with the board. They had been delighted with the results and the process and especially that they had been able to implement all the changes we recommended.

There were handshakes all around. Then, as I was being shown out, I spotted a new issue that hadn't been there originally.

In the hallway next to the cafeteria door was a big cardboard box. A garish yellow and red sign in the shape of an arrow pointed to the box, and a poster instructed people to recycle their old phones. Slogans such as "Give a second life to your old phone," "Old phone batteries are the largest energy waste," and "We send old phones to economically deprived areas" peppered the signage.

The director caught me looking at it and proudly told me that they went through so many company phones—salespeople needed the latest ones, techs and developers needed upgrades—that they were throwing out tens of thousands of pounds (that's UK monetary pounds, not weight) per month. This was their way of giving back to those unable to afford new phones. He went on for some time about how the company was being ecological, green, etc. The whole time, my mind was whirring.

At the end of his Greenpeace speech, I had just one question for him:

"So these phones are all forensically wiped, right?"

Almost immediately, he understood that hundreds of mobiles might have left the premises containing company data. We were contracted on the spot to help investigate.

The great news is that the company that came to collect the phones did an excellent job of removing all data before passing them on. Otherwise, this situation could have been a catastrophic data breach—but this good news is not why I am telling this anecdote.

There was a much more interesting issue at play, and we were allowed to do a proof of attack with the client.

You see, the cafeteria area was essentially a public space. You could walk into the reception area, and to the right of it was the café. It was not behind any security systems because it allowed visitors to be kept outside the restricted zones and meet with staff in a "safe" environment.

I have seen this setup countless times: it seems like a good solution to having to sign in guests and check who they are before meeting with them. However, in this case, the phone recycling box outside the cafeteria was located where someone could come in off the street, walk toward the cafe, grab a bunch of phones from the box, and walk back out.

We proved this several times and took approximately 30 phones without anyone watching, stopping, or interfering with us.

The phones were taken back to our lab, and we pulled data from them. Some of them were personal phones, and as soon as we confirmed that, we handed them back immediately. We only had permission to look at company property, not personal data; we didn't want to break the law.

The information we recovered from over 20 phones was astounding. Most of the phones did not require a passcode or password to gain access. (This was pre-fingerprint and biometrics, but I can tell you another time how we bypassed them.)

It remains a mystery to me why these technologically brilliant people did not understand the impact of storing all this company information on a mobile device but not taking the time to erase it before throwing the phone in a box.

Actually, that's not quite true—of the 30+ phones we found, 1 had been erased!

As we move through life, we leave digital breadcrumbs like 21st-century Hansels and Gretels, but we don't always intend to. This recycling phone box was a gold mine of information, but think about the times you have hired a rental a car using your home zip code—the next person to rent the vehicle now has that information. You never know who is getting it. The same is true when you sign into a Netflix account from an Airbnb or fill out forms on a spa weekend. What happens to the data after you leave and when it is no longer needed is a huge security weakness.

I am fortunate that my life takes me around the world: I get to travel and hire cars and stay in different places. At least 90% of the time on a trip I will delete someone else's data from a car or TV or similar. I once found a booking letter someone had left in a bathroom in a shopping mall—it included all their personal travel details. I emailed them and told them what they had done. Fifteen minutes later, I met the person and gave them the letter. They were incredibly grateful because their trip had been close to being ruined!

Look around as you go about your life, and try to spot the instances when someone else's data could be leaked. Don't be scared to ask, "What happens to that bit of paper with my details on it?" and insist that it be destroyed if the person you ask doesn't know or doesn't make a good argument. Receptionists love to jot down private information and leave it on their desks.

And finally, if you are reselling any technology, make sure you reset it back to blank/factory and keep your data safe.

Chapter 47

Fourteen Desktop PCs

By this point in the book, I hope you have gained an appreciation for physical security. If done poorly, it can undermine expensive and effective digital security controls.

That is the main reason we focus on it alongside the human side of security. When the three areas of security—human, physical, and digital—work together, you can have a robust, effective security posture. But if one of those areas is weak or missing, you can never have true security.

In my physical assessments, I often have to agree that, unlike a criminal, I will not remove computer systems that are active or plugged in.

Imagine the huge amounts of money spent protecting your computer at work: the servers that run your applications; the systems that store your client data, files, and emails—everything is physically stored somewhere, even if it's in the cloud. Those computer systems have many layers of digital protection. You need authorization and authentication to log onto them. But if you place a computer in a location with poor physical security, a criminal can pick it up and walk off with it.

It is well known that if an attacker has physical access to a computer, it is only a matter of time before they gain access to the data. And since they have taken the computer, the amount of time they have increases dramatically. They no longer have to compromise the computer in minutes before being detected; they can work on it for weeks or months.

This is why, when I perform an assessment, I look for laptops or desktops that are not plugged in or in use. While I can remove anything of value, I also have a duty of care to my clients, and removing a system that is in use could cause catastrophic effects to the business—but inactive systems are usually fair game. My work is always a balancing act between highlighting security flaws and not having detrimental side effects.

In Chapter 12, you can read about a case in which I removed a desktop PC from a client. But the following case highlights how easy it can be for me to remove large amounts of data.

I had broken into an office and found my way around the building. Many of the office spaces were packed with people and technology, but I managed to grab a few items as directed by the client.

I was on my third hour in the building and was exploring some of the less-traveled areas—these often include roofs, loft spaces, cupboards, and that kind of thing. I had been making my way up and down the building using the main staircase, but because security was roaming around, I was forced to head toward the back of the building. There I discovered a staircase that was blocked off on most of the floors.

I love finding hidden areas that are not in use. In this case, expanding certain parts of the building meant extra walls were needed, and some doorways into the stairwell had been bricked over. This is not unusual. I would say I find something like this in 1 in every 20 buildings.

The stairwell had only three working entry points, one of which was on the floor used by IT. They had been using this area for storage; as I said, the company had been expanding, and so had the IT team.

It didn't take long for me to spot this hidden in an alcove.

This was a gold mine of information!

I decided to remove all the PCs. I took them one by one to another floor I could access. In total, I moved 14 PCs. But now came the hard part: I had to remove them from the building without being noticed.

I carried the first PC to the elevator, smack bang in the middle of everyone. I left another PC propped against the stairwell door to hold it open; the other 12 were still stacked on the floor.

I moved the first PC to an unprotected exit often used by smokers for breaks, where I started a new stack.

By the time I got to the fourth PC, people had started to take notice. Eventually, the inevitable happened. "Excuse me, mate!"

After a brief explanation of my actions and some exposition about how hard my job was that day, a few of the people near the elevator took pity on me and helped me carry PCs into the elevator; another person held the door open. We moved the remaining PCs down to my new stack by the door.

Then they went above and beyond in helping me steal their data: they offered to help carry the PCs out of the building to my rental car. One by one, the PCs were taken across the parking lot and loaded into the trunk and on the back seat; one went on the front passenger seat and another in the footwell.

I also took a few laptops I had found and the items I had taken earlier.

The client's response was normal for this type of work: equally delighted and disappointed with my success.

We were instructed to look at the data on those "stolen" computer systems. We found plenty of high-value data that, had I been a criminal, would have entirely broken the company and resulted in huge fines and irreparable damage to its brand.

The IT department had been storing the computers in the stairwell because they had a backlog of decommissioned PCs and needed to wipe all company data before selling them secondhand. As for the people who helped me, it turned out they had never been given any training or education about these types of threats. I hope people like this get to read my book and learn some of these lessons before something like this happens to them.

Chapter 48

Spy Gadgets

It's not always spying and cool gadgets in my job. It's often rather boring, despite what many anecdotes in this book may lead you to believe.

Even robbing banks can get "samey" and a little boring when you do it enough.

But now and then I get to break out the cool gadgets, and those days are always more fun.

In Chapter 3, I mentioned how I used night-vision goggles on a job. They are by far my most-used cool gadget. Other normal tech I use is boring, like ultra-high-powered cameras, card cloners for badge systems, and the odd laser pointer to block a CCTV camera or turn off solar sensor-based lights.

I always carry my lock picks and other entry tools. Almost every day, I carry a Leatherman multitool that contains a myriad of things I may need. Lighters and pens are also in my pocket. I have in some cases used an endoscope camera: a long, thin camera you put under a door, like you sometimes see the FBI or Special Forces using in movies. They are relatively cheap nowadays, and I use mine for all sorts of random things like checking plumbing or even once looking at an abscessed tooth in my mouth. They are wonderfully useful.

But at one site I was asked to assess, the security called for two pieces of equipment I do not usually use: a spy camera and a cat toy!

The entrance to this building was not particularly well guarded; it was a dual set of sliding doors like you might see at a supermarket. During the day, visitors called reception via a button outside, and the reception staff activated the door. To leave, a PIR motion sensor on the inside detected people walking toward the door.

At night, the entrance was closed and locked with a single lock in the middle of the door. In addition, the building had an alarm system. A few days and nights of watching showed that the normal procedure was for someone to turn up around 8:00 a.m. and unlock the side door. A warning beep sounded, and they hurried to the reception desk and entered the alarm code to disable the alarm from going off fully. They then unlocked the main door, which opened as it detected them walking away.

I could have sneaked in behind them as they walked away, but I had a better plan.

I approached the reception area and buzzed the button. I asked for a new volunteer form, and I was let in. (This common ruse works very well in this type of building.) I stood at the counter, filling in the form with fake details while the receptionist got on with her day. I handed the form over, left, and went back to my hotel. The next day, I turned up again and got entry to the reception area. I left again.

Then I waited until the early hours of the next morning. I went to the building—everything was quiet, and not a soul was around. I quickly picked the lock to the door and slid the cat toy through the gap between the doors. Those of you who've read Chapter 37, "How to Bypass PIR Detectors," already know where this is going!

For those who haven't read it, the cat toy was a long, black, flexible rod with a small piece of elastic string and a feather attached to the end. I waved the stick back and forth until the motion sensor picked it up and opened the doors.

As soon as I walked into the reception area, the alarm warning beeps started. I didn't have long, so I vaulted over the reception counter and entered the alarm disarm code into the panel.

You may have guessed from the chapter title, but for those unfamiliar with what happened, here is how I got the code.

During the first visit, while I was filling out the form, I took a spy camera out of my pocket.

This camera was disguised as a roll-on deodorant. This device was a real plastic deodorant bottle: it had been sawed into at the bottom, and a spy camera has been fitted. The camera works by detecting motion and recording for a minute before shutting down to save power. The top can be taken off to reveal the ball, which I did in this instance.

The top was covered in roll-on deodorant to give a real look and smell. The pièce de résistance, as they say, was the addition of a hair to the ball. The idea was that no one would touch a clearly used deodorant left somewhere. I tucked it beside a plant pot on the reception desk so the cleaners wouldn't notice it, and pointed it toward the alarm panel.

The camera recorded the moment the receptionist entered the code the next morning. My retrieval of the camera allowed me to play back the video and learn the code.

As I said, it's not all about cool gadgets in my job, but boy do they come in handy when you need them!

Chapter 49
How to Steal Fingerprints

F ingerprints are the most common biometric used for the last 10 years. But why do we insist on using them? In my opinion, fingerprints are not good for commercial-grade security systems, and I will get into those opinions later; but for now, we need to understand how they are used in office and commercial systems and how to bypass them. These techniques will work on common consumer systems, but I don't want to encourage you to try them without permission.

How do fingerprints work, I mean biologically? Well, your skin secretes oils 24/7; these oils collect in your fingers' ridges (whorls, arches, and loops). Look at your finger right now; see all those lines? Each line pumps out oil, and it fills the valleys between them.

Press that finger against glass or a shiny surface. See how it leaves a perfect mirror image of the lines on your finger? If that doesn't work or it's unclear, run your hands through your hair a few times and try again.

Now you have a lovely, crystal-clear fingerprint on a shiny surface. So what?

Well, let's say you use a fingerprint to access a door in your office. Offices below a certain level of security rarely have such systems, but some do. I have come across hundreds in my role, and almost always, they have a reader next to a door where a thumb or fingerprint is scanned, and the person is let in (or not).

Your fingerprint is not photographed and stored; no, that would take up a huge amount of computer memory, and it would be hard to compare fingerprints each time. Your fingerprint is scanned, points are read on it, and those coordinates are converted into a string of numbers. It's a little fancier than that, but basically, that string of numbers is stored, and that's what is compared each time. If we had access, we could brute-force those strings of numbers and inject them into the reader, but doing so would be very difficult and would take a ton of time. There are much easier methods to bypass fingerprint readers.

The first is obvious; however, as an ethical hacker and social engineer working for a client, it is untenable. I only include it here because I have seen real criminal gangs use this tactic. It's one of the reasons I strongly advise against using fingerprint/palm scanners or even iris systems in most places. There are people who have the right fingerprint or hand or eyeball to gain access, and I have seen criminal gangs physically remove those parts from individuals to open a system. Removing a thumb is quick and easy, doesn't kill the individual, and works in 99% of cases. The manufacturers of some fingerprint readers insist that they will not work unless a pulse is detected, but they almost never stop this attack.

Some manufacturers claim they can detect whether the finger is human skin or latex, and creating a latex fingerprint will not work on those systems. But most do not differentiate.

So, let's create a latex fingerprint, and then I will share how to bypass the human-skin-detection system without cutting off someone's finger.

To do this, we need a few items and a super-important health warning: the fumes produced in this experiment can kill. Be sure you have very good ventilation and filtration and wear suitable clothing and safety wear, such as goggles and breathing apparatus. I cannot stress enough how dangerous this can be.

You need the following:
- An item containing a fingerprint from your victim
- An enclosed box of some sort (ideally airtight)
- A candle or other heat source
- A tinfoil cup, like that from a cupcake or jam tart (alternatively, half a soda can turned upside down)
- Superglue
- A small amount of warm water to help with humidity
- A laser printer (not inkjet)

- Acetate sheets for the laser printer
- A graphics program
- Liquid latex

Take the item with the fingerprint, ideally something small that will fit in your enclosed box, and place it inside the enclosed box along with a small metal dish. This item *will* be destroyed, so bear that in mind. Don't use a phone or something of value like a photograph. Get the target to touch something like a cup or a glass—anything small or that can be cut up.

Squirt a good amount of superglue into the small metal dish, and heat the metal dish with a candle or other heat source. Doing so creates very nasty white vapor that can contain cyanide, so I shouldn't need to tell you to avoid breathing these fumes. It smells incredibly bad, too!

The white vapor adheres to the oils of the fingerprint; it then hardens into a tough white "plastic," making the fingerprint visible.

You can experiment with this setup to get better results. Suspending the item above the metal dish helps avoid using too much superglue. This whole process should take between 20 and 40 seconds. Depending on your setup, it can take several minutes, so be patient. Be sure everything is safe before opening the enclosed box, and ensure that the fumes are dispersed rapidly and safely.

The item should now be covered in a thin layer of hardened superglue, and the fingerprint should be clear.

The next stage is a bit tricky. Take a very good close-up photograph, or use a scanner to capture the print. Then, import the fingerprint into a computer graphics program and convert it to black and white (not greyscale)—it should have just black and white, nothing else. You may also need to clean up the image. In the end, the lines should be white and the valleys black. To do this, you may have to invert the image. Again, use your graphics program to do this.

(When the TV show *MythBusters* showed this technique, they purposely cut out the part where you invert the image to get black valleys and white ridges. They did this to prevent this knowledge from being used).

Once you have a clear black-and-white image, print it onto the acetate sheet using a laser printer. Why is that important? Well, a laser printer places ink on top of the sheet, and a laser hardens it. With an inkjet, ink is sprayed on and absorbed into the paper. You want slightly raised "ink." When you print the fingerprint, the version on the acetate will be inverted: you can see that the valleys stick up above the sheet.

Why do you need an inverted version? Because this sheet is a mold; you need to pour the liquid latex over the fingerprint. When the latex hardens and you peel it off, the black ridges will become the valleys, and the valleys will become the original ridges of the fingerprint.

You can now cut out the latex fingerprint and use a small dab of the liquid latex to glue it over your own finger for use in the attack.

It is an incredibly easy, quick process, and with skill and experience, it can be done in less than half an hour.

Some of you may recall that I said some readers can detect latex or non-human skin. How do they do that? Well, the common method is to use electricity to measure the skin's resistance. Human skin has a different resistance than latex; it has a different resistance than all but a few things.

Instead of latex, in my fake fingerprints I often use what is known as *pig gelatine*. It's derived by boiling parts of a pig and then is dried and sold in granulated form. It's used in foods and is a yellowish color. (If you have ever had the pleasure of eating a porkpie in England, you know what it is). Pigs are used in various medical processes because a pig's organs and skin mimic those of humans. In fact, tattooists have been known to tattoo pigs for practice when learning (replica skin is generally used nowadays).

For our needs, human skin and fake pig-gelatine fingerprints have the same electrical resistance. Swapping out the latex for pig gelatine will mean a higher rate of success on more-sophisticated detectors. With enough practice, it is possible to create entire fingers or thumbs with fake internal blood vessels by using thin plastic tubing and a small pulsatile pump to mimic a body pulse and salted water to simulate sweat. More than once, our house refrigerator has been filled with fake fingers cooling in molds.

Chapter 50

Five Banks a Week

I have probably broken into more banks than anyone you will ever meet. A little boastful, perhaps, but it's probably true. Hopefully, most people will not meet anyone who has ever broken into a bank—bank robbers are few and far between, and I would like to think it is because people like me make it more difficult.

I can't count how many banks I have broken into. It's a career of decades at thousands of sites, but I can give you a small hint in terms of things I have learned about bank security and planning.

Years ago, I was commissioned by a major brand bank to perform a series of assessments against its banks. I was free to pick which branches, but the client wanted several areas checked.

Once we agreed on the branches and got all the legal paperwork taken care of, time was the most important thing: everything had to be completed by Christmas.

We had taken longer than expected to get everything squared away, so we had to break into 18 banks in under a month. Breaking into one bank a month is a hard ask, but now I had to break into at least five banks per week!

To give an idea of how crazy that is, that's more than Bonnie and Clyde broke into during their entire bank robbing "career" that spanned 21 months—they only managed 15. Same for the famous bank robber John Dillinger—he only managed 12 banks between 1933 and 1934. And it's just shy of Jessie James, who, between 1866 and 1881, only managed around 9 banks (the rest of his robberies were trains and stagecoaches)—although one of those banks may not have been him, and the 10th was the disastrous failure at the First National Bank of Northfield, Minnesota, which led to his gang's breakup. All these people were violent criminals—no one should look up to them—but they are names well-known for bank robberies. And here I was planning in one month to best them all!

Breaking into a bank is 90% planning—99% if you want to ensure that it will be perfect, and even then, things may happen that you can't plan for. A lot of reconnaissance needs to be done for each bank; plans must be drawn up and meticulously considered. Another issue is that unlike criminals, we have to stay within the law. And a ton of other things must be taken into account, like backup plans, emergency backups, etc. A lot can go wrong with breaking into a bank. We are also not to disrupt the bank's operations in any way, so we have to keep breakages to a minimum.

It would normally take weeks of planning, and each bank would need its own plan. But with so many banks to be broken into, I had to come up with a single plan that could work for all the sites. I only had rough site maps and zero time to do any recon beyond using Google Street View. This approach weakened my chances, but it saved me a lot of planning time.

By the middle of the first week, I was somehow running at 100% success, having achieved all the goals the client needed. It was not looking good for them, and I was optimistic—I might pull it off after all!

The client decided things were going too well. After a quick meeting, I was directed to—well, asked nicely if we could—change the strategy. The single plan to get into the banks was apparently working too well. It was safe to assume that every one of the banks left would be susceptible to this attack, so the client would not gain more information if I repeated it. I had to begrudgingly agree.

I went back to the drawing board: each bank now needed its own plan of attack. I spent a very long weekend plotting and thinking through different operations. With minimal time, I had to figure a way in and then think on my feet each day, which was way outside my comfort zone. The chance of success looked very slim.

During this weekend, I was staying in a hotel on the outskirts of London. It was very light on provided services. There was no room service—the hotel had a well-stocked vending machine, but I needed more. I checked out local eateries and found that the near-est one would close soon. So I rushed out of the room and went to eat some awful pizza. In my hurry, I left everything mid-use; the room looked like a heist movie scene when I came back. There were photos of the banks on the sideboard and maps and layouts strewn over the bed. Beside the bed were my scribbled notes on how to rob this bank. All it needed was one of those maps with red string. I almost burst out laughing. I was glad the hotel didn't have room service, or I am sure the police would have been called.

Planning any bank heist is tricky; planning several on the fly was even harder. Due to my experience, I was able to achieve eve-rything the client needed in that hellish month. But what lessons did I learn? And, more important, why am I telling you about this?

It is easy to think that security is a simple task: stop the bad guys. But there is always a balance between risk and likelihood. You also have to consider the budget. How much is it worth spending versus how much might be taken? Obviously, the safety of the pub-lic and customers must always come first.

Banks are a fine balance of these things factors. The 18 banks I broke into all had flaws—most of them had multiple flaws. My job is not about showing up the client but rather about helping them achieve a better balance and fix their flaws. These banks represented a gigantic task, but as with any skill, the more you understand the foundations of what you are trying to do, the easier it becomes.

It's also important to remember that perfection is the enemy of good. In this case, the single flaw could be leveraged multiple ways. I didn't need to create the perfect plan for each bank. I just needed a good enough plan that could be used on multiple targets.

When performing your own assessments, do not try to come up with the perfect plan. You will find that the situation on the ground can change and ruin any plans you have. Learn to think on your feet; and, most important, do not be scared of trying new things.

Chapter 51

Finding Out Too Much

My job sometimes puts me in awkward positions, like the time I was climbing down an elevator shaft or when I was running away from security staff and happened upon a porn shoot after I jumped a garden fence. There was the time I kidnapped someone (as described in Chapter 11) and had to explain to them what I was doing. And the time I ended up huddled under a table, waiting for staff to leave, and they didn't leave for an hour. I've spent significant time in ditches, in bushes, up trees, and on roofs in the rain and snow. Once I hid under a car in a parking garage, and I've hidden in closets and squeezed awkwardly into turnstiles with people (see Chapter 66). But nothing prepared me for what happened the day I found out way too much.

I had been tasked with getting into a large, well-known commercial company. The building was situated on a grand British country estate. Lush greenery surrounded the amazing structure, which had been taken over by the company decades before. The golden cream brickwork dated back centuries. The long driveway ended in a circular area for dropping off—I assumed it fitted the dimensions required for horse-drawn carriages to turn back when the building was built. To the right was a smaller gravel drive leading to the side of the building where cars could park. Several expensive cars sat in the parking area, each parking spot had a white hand-painted sign indicating who was allowed to park there.

Beyond this was another, larger parking area that I assumed was for the 40 or so staff members who worked there, judging from the much less flashy motors.

Gaining access was a breeze, with basically no security anywhere because of the frequently encountered "Who would want to attack us?" mindset that is so dangerous.

I spent the next hour or two performing all the tasks the board of directors had hired me to do. The place was as open as almost any I had ever encountered.

The staff were overpaid and under-educated about security. Helpful to a tee, they assisted me in performing actions that would have taken down the company, had I been a real criminal.

When I am given a set of tasks to perform, the client often assumes that I will be caught and not achieve anything, so getting them to agree to more tasks is a fight. Why give me four tasks if I won't even get into the building? Why bother asking me to do something impossible when I will certainly be caught once I am in? But this client knew I would get in, and they knew I would achieve every goal; it felt as though they were just confirming what they already knew. Weird.

Toward the end of my tasks, I happened upon the directors' offices, which were guarded by a single personal assistant (PA) who sat to one side of the entrance. I saw that both directors were out and that there was a pile of mail on the PA's desk.

I decided to act like a bumbling newcomer. I approached the woman and acted nervous—I dropped my pen and then my notebook. I stood chatting with her about the directors and the computer I was meant to be checking on. She said the directors were out playing golf but would be back soon, so I could not go in. She wouldn't allow me to enter without their permission, or they might fire her. No one crossed them.

I told her I would be back later and dropped my notebook again.

I walked out carrying a bunch of mail. Most of it was already opened, but two letters had handwritten names with no address and were unopened. I had scooped up the mail by dropping my notebook on the letters and picking them up with it. The receptionist never noticed.

At the end of the day, I sat in a meeting room and called my clients. I told them about everything, including that I was able to remove some mail from the directors' PA. One of the board members chuckled when he heard what I had. He then directed me to open one of the handwritten letters.

It read as follows:

Dear ******,

I regret to inform you that despite multiple warnings, and due to your over-exuberance in spending our money, proclivity for golf over business, and lack of concern about security and the welfare of company property, you are to be relieved of your role immediately.

Sincerely,

Board of Directors

It was signed by the entire board. They had decided the fate of the director before I even finished the job. No wonder the job felt like they already knew how bad the situation was; this test would be the death knell underlying the decision. I don't feel good about people losing their roles because of me; I would rather they were given proper training and education. But in this case, the decision was made before I was even involved.

Incidentally, this is a good place to point out a major difference between me and a criminal: I abide by a code of ethics. The information I had in my hand had yet to reach the directors. That meant the stock market would be unaffected by the news. I could have shorted the stock in the company, knowing the news would negatively affect its stock price before rebounding. With my insider knowledge, I could have made a fortune.

Chapter 52

Needle in a Haystack

Human behavior is fascinating. We have social rules and ways of working that baffle me as a security expert. We often find it helpful to go along with traditions and conventions that, when you step back and look at them, are not healthy or secure. I guess it comes from our innate desire to be connected to something bigger than ourselves—to know we are not alone in the universe or here on Earth.

A lot of what I do is taking advantage of human nature and behaviors, those societal norms that hinder security.

For instance, consider tailgating: the act of following someone through a door or barrier. Attackers often do this to gain access to areas they are restricted from entering. You have probably done this yourself, albeit not to break in somewhere but because you forgot your pass.

Picture this scenario: You are coming back from lunch, and as you approach the office, a colleague is just ahead of you. They swipe their pass and open the door. They look back at you and step away, and you smile at them. They hold the door open for you as you do that awkward half-run, grab the door, and say thanks. I am sure that or something similar has happened to everyone at some point.

It's a great example of human nature and social norms subverting security! From a human side, your colleague was polite and kind when they helped you. From a security side, they let a stranger into the building and subverted security controls. The right thing for them to do for security was to close the door and force you to use your pass.

It's hard to see why it matters, but if a criminal gets into a building, they are through the strongest defense line. This book is full of anecdotes about me doing things that could have been catastrophic if a criminal had done them. By *catastrophic*, I mean the company could lose millions, personal data could be leaked, human lives or companies could be ruined, and people could lose their jobs or worse. I take advantage of human nature and its biases to help me achieve my goals in these assessments.

Take, for instance, the time I was asked by a client to infiltrate their company and locate and, if possible, remove four folders that contained sensitive documentation. The client was under the illusion that I would not be able to get in, let alone find these documents, as the company had thousands of folders in many, many closets over many floors.

I met my client on a side road next to the target building. He was there to observe and, I think, gloat a little. A little over 15 minutes later, I approached him with the target document folders in my arms. He was not gloating now but was in utter shock.

He was dumbfounded about how I could have gained access to the building, found these four hidden folders, and removed them within such a short time.

How I got in and out is not what I want to highlight here—those methods are covered in several other chapters of this book. The more important thing to know is how quickly I found the four folders.

It doesn't take long to wander around a whole floor looking in closets—maybe slightly longer if you are being sneaky, but still only a few minutes per floor. He wasn't kidding when he said they had tens of thousands of folders that were impressively sorted into closets. For every folder on someone's desk, there was a marker in the appropriate closet, saying who had the folder.

How do you find four needles in a multi-floor haystack? Well, let me introduce you to human nature. Actually, it's better if I show you.

Once you see them in place, you can tell how I found them so quickly. I initially saw them from several rows away, like beacons in a night-time raid. Humans love to highlight things as important, and among the thousands of boring black folders over several floors, these were the only four folders that stood out.

For reasons we will mark up to human evolution, red signifies something to pay attention to. Poisonous animals and plants are often red as a warning; our hazard alarms and warning and stop signals are all red. Red is *the* color to pay attention to.

So, by making these special folders red, it made it obvious to anyone that they were the ultimate folders in the whole building— they must be paid attention to.

As you can see, that small bias of human nature did not, in fact, help the company's security. These four red folders were obvious to me, an attacker, and would be as obvious to a criminal.

It's very easy to find four needles in a multi-floor haystack when the needles are painted bright red!

It's also important to note that no one stopped me from removing the folders. This again was human nature in action. Everyone in the company knew the red files were important: most never got to see or use them because they were so important. So anyone holding one must be very important, right? I mean, why else would anyone have them? As soon as I picked up the folders, I became someone allowed to have them. As I walked down the stairs past countless people, no one dared to stop me and ask where I was going with them.

Because of human bias, I was able to walk out the front door and over to my client, cradling my haul.

Chapter 53

Stealing a Purse and Keys

I remove a lot of business-related assets during assessments, things like laptops or computers that are discarded or turned off. My work is about highlighting the company's security, not the individuals.

A person can be easily manipulated or avoided, and equipment can be manipulated or avoided or even disabled, but a company's security culture can overcome those attacks. It is much more difficult to subvert multiple security mechanisms or manipulate multiple people. Security is best applied in layers rather than using a single factor. We gave up single-walled castles in the Middle Ages, and we cannot rely on that approach today.

There are times, though, when a single individual holds more power and has more access than others. How do we assess an individual? And when should we do so?

When a large bank or secure firm is targeted by an organized crime group or violent gang, the attackers may target an individual such as a CEO or other executive with power and access. While this is a horrible topic, it's one that we must deal with and simulate for people who are likely to be targeted in what we call *executive assurance*.

As I have mentioned many times in this book, as security professionals, we do not perform violence, but we can simulate the stages before such an attack would take place. This is often referred to as the *recon stage* and can be a legal minefield, so please be careful and understand the laws and requirements for you and the client.

I was once targeting an individual for executive assurance. As part of this operation, we had to gain access to what would normally be considered a private space: their car. I checked the local laws, and the company owned the vehicle. Nowadays, there are a hundred ways to get into a vehicle without leaving a trace; back when this was done, the easiest method was to use the keys. However, the keys were always with the target.

I managed to infiltrate the target's office space, and after creating a small diversion, I hoped to find her bag and remove the keys to the vehicle. The issue was that credit-card-style keys were introduced in the 2000s, and I didn't know this would be the style of key before delving into the bag.

I had only a moment to decide what to do, so I removed her entire purse, hoping to find the keys later and return the whole thing intact.

As a result, I ended up walking around the office trying to get out while holding a large, bright pink purse, which is not the most subtle way to remove an item.

Once out of the building, I had to locate the target's car. A quick look through her purse found the credit-card key to a Mercedes Benz. I tried each Mercedes until I gained access. Like most people, she had left a veritable treasure trove of items in the vehicle, which I removed.

By the end of the day, I had gathered enough documents, photographs, bills, and information from this person that I was confident going into the washup meeting and describing in detail how a criminal organization would target her.

Obviously, this is not the only executive assurance I've performed. While I understand the need for a human to decorate their workspace with personal items and assume their workspace is secure, it never fails to shock me that people are blatant with their belongings. I have found amazing things on people's desks—or in their company vehicles or lockers—that relate to their private lives.

The point of this small insight is that you should be wary of leaving objects that could be valuable to an attacker in places you think are secure rather than places that actually are secure.

People often believe you have to be paranoid to be secure, but this is not a great way to live. Having a healthy suspicion of people and places and understanding situational awareness could save your life, not just improve your security.

Chapter 54

How to Pick Locks

Picking locks is nothing like you see in the movies. It's hilarious to watch movies and TV shows attempt their versions of picking a lock. Very few people seem to know how it works, yet it is incredibly easy to do and a fun pastime.

Picking locks is much like golf; it's easy to understand the principles and even relatively simple to start once you have the right equipment. You will then spend the rest of your life trying to get better at it. Unlike golf, though, it can be practiced all year; you can do it anywhere—a train, a plane, a bus ride, in the park, in bed, or even on the toilet. All you need are some lock picks and something to pick!

First let's look at the tools, and then we'll get into how to use them.

You will need, obviously, something to pick. I suggest a cheap padlock to get started.

Then you need a lock-picking kit. When I began doing this as a kid, I made my own from old street sweeper blades I found on the streets in London. I made them for others, too. But let's be honest: we have moved on, and lock-pick kits are now dirt cheap and available almost everywhere (including Amazon).

Before you buy a kit, though, take a quick look at your local laws. In some places, owning, carrying, or even selling lock picks can be illegal. In other places, you may only have them if they're required for your work. Please be careful before buying or making lock picks.

There are many types of lock picks, but I'm not going into each type here. There are wonderful books on this subject; this chapter is just a taster.

To pick a lock, you need two tools: a *picker* and a *turner*, also known as a *tension tool*. The picker does the actual picking, and the tension tool provides a small turning force.

To understand what you are going to do, grab a key and a lock, and let's look at them together.

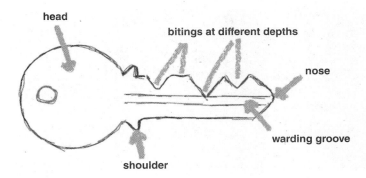

A key has bumps and dips (the *biting* or *teeth*) as you look along the length. Toward the part you hold is a big stopper (called the *collar* or *shoulder*). This prevents the key from going too far into the lock and helps align everything. Also note that the key has a funny shape if you look directly down at it; this is called the *warding*. Each lock has a different warding that matches the key so you can't accidentally use the wrong key. To pick a lock, you can essentially ignore the warding; it won't prevent a lock pick from going in.

Looking at a lock from the outside won't tell you much other than the matching warding to the key; try putting in different keys and seeing how the real key fits versus other keys. You might even find a key with a matching warding, but it still won't turn the lock. Why? Well, inside the lock is a series of *pins* and *cylinders*.

A circular part rotates when you turn the real key; the main body remains in place. Much like a padlock, a solid bit of metal prevents the inner circular part (the *core*) from turning in the body. Those solid parts are the pins.

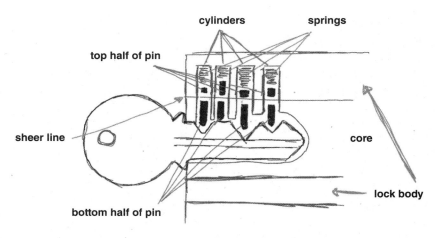

(gaps have been exaggerated)

A pin is made of two parts, and those two parts can only move up and down inside a cylinder. A spring pushes them down, and because the break in the pin doesn't match up precisely with the join of the core and the body, it prevents the circular core from rotating.

To pick a lock, you have to push each pin up just the tiniest amount to perfectly align the break in the pin. A key does this by having those dips and ridges; each pin sits on its ridge and perfectly aligns the breakpoints. Then you can apply a turning force to the core, and the lock opens.

Sounds easy, right? It is, with practice, but you aren't dealing with just one pin—it's often a minimum of four pins. It's also common to have six or sometimes up to eight pins. I won't get into the fancy security systems used in some very expensive locks; we are, after all, just getting started on this road to your new hobby. So, let's say your first lock has only six pins to worry about. How do you pick it?

If you use your pick to push the first pin up to the right place, how do you keep it hovering in space with the spring pushing it down while you move the next one? You can take advantage of the tiny imperfections in how they are made.

If you apply a very small turning force using your tension tool, one pin will hit the boundary first and prevent the lock from turning. Great: you didn't open it. What a waste of time, huh?

No, because only one of the six pins prevents it from turning a fraction more, and you found which one! Now you put in your pick tool and gently push each pin until you find the pin that is *binding* the lock. It will be obvious because it won't move (you're stopping it with the turning force). The rest are sitting on their tiny springs. Push that bound pin until you hear a tiny click or the core turns a tiny bit. It will stop on the next pin that is binding.

Repeat that process for all the pins, each one allowing the next pin to bind until you get to the last pin and nothing stops it from moving. You have unlocked your first lock! Congratulations.

While I say this is easy, it takes practice and patience. If you apply too much pressure to the tension tool, it will not work, and you might even break it!

I strongly encourage you to take this up as a hobby, even if you have no intention of ever doing a job similar to mine. The skill could save your life. I have helped many people gain access to their own homes and buildings without resorting to expensive locksmiths or damaging a window.

If you are not interested about learning the skill, other methods to pick a lock can be faster. One method, called *raking* (you will have a rake in your pick kit), works on many locks (even some high-security ones).

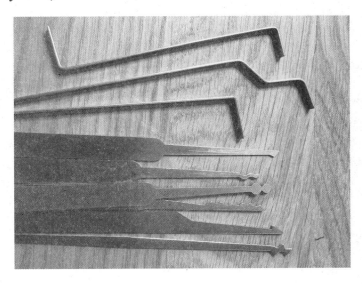

Another method, *bumping*, uses special bump keys (as mentioned in Chapter 42). While it takes a certain amount of practice, it can be awesomely effective.

My favourite type of picks are *comb* picks. I have used these to open many locks and even won a couple of contests that didn't bar their use. A comb pick aligns long prongs with each of the pins, similar to the key; however, you can then push the pins all the way out of the core cylinder and up into the space where the spring is, essentially bypassing the pins altogether.

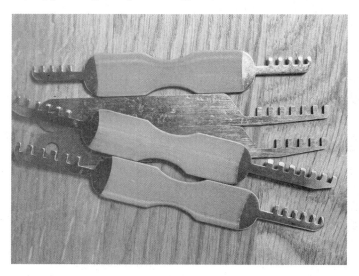

Finally, you have lock pick guns, either manual or automatic. These work by flicking all the pins up rapidly and letting you use the short time when they are all pushed out of the way, like the comb pick, to turn the lock.

Chapter 55

The Porn Cupboard

Every now and then, something weird happens during my work that feels like an absurd scene in a movie and makes me stop and think about my life choices.

This anecdote is a small part of what happened in just one week in a particular office in the middle of England. I can't share most of that week, mostly because of client privilege but also because I am not sure you would believe me if I described the even crazier moments—like the day I was running away from a security guard and, after jumping over a fence, landed in a garden where a pornographic movie was being shot. You can picture this scenario if you cross the fence scene in *Hot Fuzz* with the scene in *Ferris Bueller's Day Off*.

As I said, this was not even the weirdest thing that happened that week. However, I want to tell you about the cupboard.

With most break-ins that I perform, it is nice to find a safe space I can use to rest, call in support, or plot and scheme and go over notes. Often that place is a restroom, because people tend to stay away from them and don't ask questions when you leave them.

So, I found myself sitting in a cubicle at the end of the row, door locked and seat down, plotting my next move.

A childhood incident affected my sense of smell, but even so, the smell of chemical cleaners was a little overpowering even for me. I resolved to keep my visits to my "office" as short as possible.

As part of my job infiltrating buildings, I note things that others do not. I am constantly looking for ways in and out of buildings that an attacker or myself could take advantage of. I have often located hidden stairwells, doors to interesting places, and areas not known to anyone.

Because of this sense of exploration, I noticed that the cubicle I was in had a panel opening about three feet high and two feet wide. It was a hinged door held shut with a small screw; on closer inspection, that screw didn't look well secured.

I always carry a multitool with me for times like this, but in this case, I was able to pry the door open with no issues—the screw didn't attach to anything! The door was held shut by a small magnet like you would see in a kitchen cupboard. There was also a piece of fishing line attached to a switch. I assumed it was a broken light or something similar.

I pulled the door open and shone a flashlight inside. Maybe I could squeeze in; who knew where this false wall could lead?

The light illuminated a small shelf an arm's reach away. The shelf held a stack of 10 or 12 pornographic magazines. I threw up a little in my mouth as my brain put together the puzzle of the cupboard, the cubicle, and the magazines.

I slammed the door shut and bolted from the toilet to catch my breath and consider where my next office would be. I slinked around the corner to the mini kitchenette and grabbed a cup of water.

Within about 30 seconds of me getting my water and catching my breath, five or six security guards ran past the kitchen and barrelled into the toilets like a SWAT team making a high-end drug bust. The chaos attracted the employees' attention, and we were all gawking at the toilet door as the men inside kicked open cubicle doors and shouted.

I knew the toilets were empty. What the hell had just happened? As with any security incident, I decided not to hang around to find out.

Some hours later, during a washup meeting with the client, I learned that I had triggered a sting operation that had been planned for weeks.

The cupboard had been discovered months ago by staff, and security had been alerted. Rather than remove the items and move on, the security team had rigged up some fishing line connected to a remote that would alert them when the offending occupant opened the door. After a week of waiting with no avail, the door was suddenly triggered when I inadvertently took a peek. The SWAT-like response was not for me but for the cupboard. Sometimes you shouldn't open cupboards, especially those in toilets. I have no idea if the offending person was ever caught, but I wonder what the plan was if they had been caught red-handed?

Chapter 56

The Apartment Across the Way

Most of the time when doing recon, I have to sit in ditches, hide in trees, or stand around in the cold for hours. But one time, the planets aligned, and I lucked out by finding an apartment block across from the target site with serviced apartments rentable by the day.

For this job, I formulated a plan: I would rent an apartment in the block across the street to perform my recon. Bonus points because I could stay warm and do all my recon from the comfort of a sofa. I could sit and eat and, more importantly, not be seen or raise suspicion, which meant I could do many more hours of recon than usual. This was going to be a proper stakeout!

As with any plan, there are simple parts and there are complicated parts you can't always control. The tricky part of this plan would be booking the right apartment, because only three had windows facing the dull grey building I needed to break into; the rest looked out onto a lovely vista. The booking system didn't allow you to pick a specific apartment; you were assigned whichever one was free. So, a few options came to mind. I could, for example, have wasted a lot of the client's budget booking several apartments and hoping one of them would work, but my travel department had a much better idea. She was going to get me the apartment I needed!

I am known for my social engineering exploits—this book is a testament to some of those escapades, after all. But the plan my travel assistant came up with still blows my mind; I would never have thought of it.

She concocted an amazing story. She called the booking company and explained that she was booking an apartment on my behalf and that I needed a very specific room. She was told that company policy prohibited doing that and bookings were on a first-come, first-served basis because people always wanted the lovely view offered by the other side of the building—opposite the one I needed.

My assistant then switched to her cunning plan and pulled on the heartstrings of the lady at the booking company who was on the phone. The story was that I needed the apartment overlooking the building because my girlfriend worked there, and I worked abroad. I planned to surprise her by flying in the night before and then watch and wait until I saw her leave for lunch so I could rush out to meet her and propose marriage right there on the corner. Part of the story included where we met before going on our first date.

Obviously, none of that was true. It sounds like a horrible way to propose, but the lady from the apartment's booking department was sold. She gushed at how romantic it all was and decided that maybe she could make an exception just this once. That is how I was booked into the second-floor apartment overlooking the entrance to the target.

It got even better: when I arrived for my stakeout, sitting on the table in the living room was a lovely bunch of flowers alongside a bottle of champagne—both on the house. There was also a note wishing me luck from the booking team. How lovely was that?

The apartment location gave me the perfect place to spend a few days with a high-powered camera. I took photos of almost all of the staff and their badges. I wrote down in my notebook the times when people came and went. Because I could sit undetected and undisturbed, it was amazing how much I managed to glean about their office life.

Here is a photo of one of the employees I recorded over four days.

From watching and my notes, I learned that he took two breaks per day. Each time, he left the building by the same exit point, walked up the street to the corner shop to buy a few items (often a paper in the morning), and then walked back. His lunch break was taken mostly at the same time each day, and that took him in the opposite direction to a nearby greasy-spoon café. I also noted that he was always a little late coming back compared to other employees.

As you can see in the photo, every time he left the building, he had his badge proudly around his neck. On it was a wealth of information.

The image you see here is one of the many wide-angle shots I took. I am sharing this one as I don't want to give away too much to you. But I was able to take multiple very close-up shots of this man's badge. To give you an idea of how fantastic my stakeout spot was, I had 7 or 8 opportunities per day (28 in total because of his breaks), and each time, I took 20 or so photographs. So, for this employee, I took between 200–500 photos.

As you can imagine, I was able to build a very clear image of the company's badge system. Imagine if someone watched you for four days and took hundreds of photographs of you: they could get a lot of information!

After several days of recon, I spent a day designing and replicating a badge based on his and many other staff badges. Donning my fake badge, I was able to walk into the building with no drama whatsoever. The badge was checked out by several security guards throughout the assessment and passed inspection. I even took a chance and used it successfully at the company's other building.

I never like to create one-off things, so I made five fake badges in case I lost one or needed backups. When I spoke with the client at the end of the assessment, they carefully inspected every badge. They were shocked at the tiny details I had replicated. The five badges I had made were so believable that when I finished, the client asked to keep them as they were having issues getting new badges made quickly enough, and those five could be used immediately for new staff.

Chapter 57

Magazine Shoot

My work may seem like a lot of fun at the expense of a client, but it obviously has to have a point. The end result of an assessment is to improve security, and during the assessment, I am there to find the baseline lowest security awareness.

Let me explain that a little.

I hope you can see that a company where I can enter, remove items, and leave without security intercepting me has a worse security posture than one that, say, prevents me from removing an item or accessing a specific area. *Security posture* is your readiness to prevent a security breach, whether digital or physical.

My job on site is not just to get in. It is to find the lowest point of that security posture. What is the least effort required to perform the action expected? That is, what can I get away with? It is not just a question of getting in, because time is always on the attacker's side.

I have been doing this for almost three decades, and I have a 100% success rate at gaining access. Does that mean I am the world's best? No, it means I strategically pick my opportunity to take advantage of security issues, and that can require some time to do. As a result, the attack I perform will not always work. The other disadvantage of gaining access is that the client only learns about a single flaw: say, one window that was a weak point that day, or one time a gate was left ajar too long. It does not give them an overall holistic view of their security.

To understand a client's security posture, I tell them not to focus on the "getting in" part; we assume that will happen. I focus on finding the thing I need to do to get employees to notice my actions. Is that "thing" walking around the site without a badge? Is it taking items or plugging things in? Is it taking photographs in restricted areas? Each of these will give an understanding of the company's security posture. The more I can get away with, the lower that posture.

You can visualize this better if you imagine three small houses: one guarded by the military, one by a security guard, and one by an unpaid volunteer. Now imagine that you attack each house with three different attack methods: first with a gun, second with a base-ball bat, and third with screaming and fists. Each house has a secu-rity posture, and you can imagine each house's responses to three attack styles. The military posture will prevent all attacks; the secu-rity guard will prevent attacks up to the baseball bat, and the unpaid volunteer will maybe prevent the attack with fists. This shows you the minimum attack you would need to perform on each house.

I have a wonderful anecdote about trying to find a client's secu-rity posture and would love to share it with you.

I was given a list of tasks to perform on a government building that was very well protected (not armed guards, though). The client and I arranged for me to perform a series of attacks over a whole week. But the client had one caveat: I had to break in a different way each day!

To provide proof to a client that I have obtained access to certain locations, it is often easiest to take a photograph. This also allows me to prove stuff such as unlocked desktops, violations of a clear-desk policy, etc. During this week-long attack on the site, it became clear that the site's security posture was very low. On one occasion, I compromised a building via a well-guarded rear access point. Once I was in, I decided to have some fun by exiting the building via the main reception. As I was leaving, I mentioned to the recep-tionist that I was popping out to my car to get my camera and asked if she would mind letting me back in when I returned, as my pass was upstairs. Even though we had never met, she immediately said, "Yes, of course." I went to my car and picked up a huge SLR camera with a heavy zoom lens. Then I walked back to the building, and, as expected, the receptionist opened the door. This was not surprising, given the security posture of the rest of the building.

I took my camera on a tour of the different floors, taking photos as I moved around. Eventually I went to the finance floor to take the photos I needed as proof of unlocked desktops, etc.; and as I had not yet been accosted, I decided to see how much I could get away with. I brazenly stood in the middle of the massive floor and started snapping away. No one asked what I was doing, so I tried new things to see when people would notice. I ended up standing on a rotating stool, which was very much a health and safety risk and not something someone would normally do in an office. It was only when I did this that I was approached: a lady popped seemingly out of nowhere and said, "Excuse me!" I spun around. "Excuse me . . . are . . . are we going to be in a magazine?" I stifled my laughter and, with a straight face, replied, "Well, in a way. It'll go in a document of sorts." She was excited, and she and her colleagues started posing for additional photos.

I am not sure if they ever got to see the final report about their behavior and the security posture of the site, but I am pretty sure they would have been embarrassed about the outcome. Hopefully they got the training and education they needed to help improve the situation. The point of this anecdote is to help you understand why it's important for you to identify behaviors and people that are not supposed to be around you. Situational awareness is helpful for both your personal safety and the security of the company you work for.

Chapter 58

Double Trouble

Rarely in my job do I come close to simulating criminal behavior. Obviously, I break into places, remove items, etc. However, there are things criminals are known to do that I will never replicate. One of those is violence. Violence against anyone is unacceptable, nor can it be accepted by any contract—never allow a client to railroad you into breaking the law.

With that said, sometimes you can simulate things like violence without performing them. I worked with a client many years ago that had security guards armed with batons and electric tasers. This posed a challenge because to physically overwhelm those people, a criminal would need greater force. This, unfortunately, would mean a firearm.

I would never even use a dummy firearm on a client site. How do you simulate the use of a firearm without having any analogue of one? The simple answer is a letter.

I want to focus on one particular well-guarded area of the site to show you how simulated violence can be implemented.

Imagine a large concrete building with a very large steel door that has a tiny armored window. Behind this steel door was a small L-shaped room. In that room were two armed guards, two seats, and a desk with a communication system to the outside door. On the opposite side of the room was a bright red steel door that looked like something from a sci-fi movie.

My tasks included gaining access to the room behind the red door. Getting into the first room would be challenging; and the armed guards would not be easily persuaded to let me past the second, that was for sure.

I approached the outer door, pressed the intercom button, and got the immediate attention of the guards inside. This is where the tricks started. Once the intercom sparked to life, I moved my lips without making a sound to simulate audio failure. I also continually half-pressed the intercom button to create electrical interference. You've likely seen this type of behavior in comedy movies or when the movie hero pretends to have a poor connection with their superiors so they can ignore an order. Despite this movie trope being so well-known in real life, it works surprisingly well. The first guard quickly became frustrated. I held a letter up to the camera for him to try to read (I knew he wouldn't be able to). I pointed at the letter and made angry-looking faces and mouth movements.

Within 30 seconds, the first door popped open, and the angry guard stepped into the gap. I handed him the letter and saw his face change as he read it. So, what did it say?

Dear reader,

You have been handed a letter by an operative who has been instructed by {client} to perform an assessment of the security of the {censored} facility. This is a simulated attack; however, you must abide by the instructions below.

- *Secure the facility, and call {censored} to confirm the operative's name and company along with the validity of this letter.*
- *Once validation has happened, please confirm the rest of the instructions that follow. Do not deviate from these instructions, to ensure the continued security of the {censored} facility.*
- *Instruct all personnel in the security room that the operative outside has a simulated firearm and has forcibly gained entry into the facility and the operative's instructions must be followed.*
- *Allow the operative to enter the security room.*
- *Perform actions as instructed by the operative.*

The rest of the letter laid out a few other pieces that I have removed for client confidentiality, but the bulk of the idea is shown.

I was able to use this letter to gain access to the red door without actual violence because the client enabled the security personnel and me to perform actions that would only happen if criminals escalated the violence level to overcome the security guards.

Never underestimate the power of a letter alongside a client willing to try new things.

Chapter 59

Fake ID

When I say "fake ID," people think of one of two types: the type underage people use to be served alcohol or get into clubs; or a fake passport and the persona that comes with it, as in a spy movie where the villain or hero is given a brown envelope containing a new ID.

Those are not the types I am talking about here. Doing either of those will get you into serious trouble, and I strongly suggest you don't even try.

I am talking about the sort of ID that impersonates your client or someone they will trust.

Corporate IDs can take many forms, but in recent years I have found that most are credit-card-sized plastic with color printing, often held in a plastic badge holder and attached to a lanyard. Before this, there were dozens of different types, materials, and ways to attach the ID, which caused me trouble. I had to work out what the ID looked like, what materials to use, how to appropriately wear it,, etc. Once I had to work out a complex color scheme used by a company, to ensure that I matched their system and didn't stand out. The various colors worked different days and shifts: wearing a badge with an orange border would have stood out on a Tuesday but not on a Wednesday, and badges with a purple lanyard on the shop floor would have stood out, unlike a blue lanyard. Badge systems can be complicated, and from a security point of view, that's a good thing; it makes my job harder, and the criminals' jobs harder, too.

Back in the day, before every company had ID cards, there were other ways to fake ID. Let me share a funny anecdote that still makes me chuckle today.

I was tasked with testing the security of a company that had multiple buildings in one city. The main target was a small, uninteresting-looking building—squat and boring, as the most interesting places normally are. (They were built by governments to be somewhat warproof and to blend into the background as much as possible.)

Inside this concrete building was a small room that housed a very important computer that had to be kept secure. Gaining access to the building was going to be an impossible task, let alone accessing that room. I needed a legitimate ID, but there were none to forge; access was all done based on face-to-face trust. And unlike in the amazing movie *Face/Off,* starring Nicolas Cage and John Travolta, I did not have access to a fake face.

I did what anyone confronted with the unsurmountable task of breaking into a building using impossible-to-replicate ID would have done: I broke into an entirely different building.

Getting into the less-secure building was a challenge, but that is not the point of this anecdote. I managed to track down some names of people who might have had access to the room I needed in the other building. I spent the next few hours stalking around the building, trying to locate them. After what felt like forever, I found one chap's office; he was not in, so his desk was empty. Let's call this person Mark Target to protect everyone's anonymity.

I approached the desk and asked someone sitting nearby if Mark was available, and they responded that he was not around. I politely asked if he had a business card, something not many people carry today: a small card giving contact details such as name, job title, and phone number. I was pointed to a small box on Mark's desk, and I took several cards.

After some pleasantries, I made my exit and headed across the city to the more secure location. I buzzed into the main reception, walked in, and was asked by the security guard who I was.

"Mark Target."

He looked at me like a dog that didn't understand its owner. I started to panic a little inside. "You're not Mark! Really? You're Mark?"

I had no idea what was going on, so I went with it. "Yes, I am, really." At this point, I grabbed my small pack of stolen business cards and handed him one, making sure he saw that they were all for the same person first and not just a selection of cards. His demeanor changed instantly. He became the most friendly security guard I have ever encountered; he was delighted to see me. He shook my hand enthusiastically and said it was great to see me. "How are the kids?" he asked.

"Erm, great, I guess!"

We chatted for a few moments, him asking random questions and me doing my best to deflect them or answer in a way I felt was appropriate. He then asked, "What can I do for you?"

"Well," I said, "I could really use access to the (censored) today if that's at all possible." I felt that asking outright would be the best way forward—go big or go home, right?

He stared at me blankly, as if I had asked something so ridiculous that he couldn't believe it. We looked at each other for what felt like minutes.

Suddenly he grabbed my shoulder and said, "For you, my friend, anything—anything at all. Come this way!" He dragged me into the secure room and asked if I needed anything else.

He walked away, promising to bring me some tea and telling me to shout if I wanted anything. I sat in front of the terminal in shock: how on earth did that happen, and why?

Several hours later, during my washup meeting with the client, I described these events. They couldn't believe it, so we all got in the car and drove to the site. There in the reception room was the same security guard, and again he greeted me like an old friend, "Mark, my dear friend, twice in a day—what a pleasure!"

After some explanation of who I was and what I was doing, he seemed a little more crestfallen than expected. It transpired that the real Mark called this office once a week to get some statistics from the guard, and over many years they had struck up a quasi-friendship. They had talked about everything and anything over the years. The weird thing was that despite working just miles apart and having a good friendship, they had never met face to face! Today the security guard thought his friend Mark had final found a reason to come over and meet up—utterly bonkers, but totally true. When I arrived, he didn't think I was real because I didn't sound the same on the phone. The show of producing the business cards convinced him that his pal was standing in front of him.

I have it on good authority that Mark and the guard met up shortly after this incident, for real this time. I am glad I played a part in making that friendship a little stronger.

Chapter 60

Impersonation

There are certain people you are not allowed to impersonate by law, including police, firemen, and ambulance staff. Additionally, we do not impersonate anyone if doing so may cause distress to the client staff or the general public. Imagine someone walking into a building dressed as a member of a bomb squad and demanding that everyone leave. Effective, for sure, but even with permission from the building owners, it would cause undue distress. Likewise, certain actions could lead to injury: walking into a building and setting off a fire alarm, for instance, or shutting off the power or water. All these actions would be effective but would cause harm and stress, so we do not do those (or similar) things. I try not to impersonate anyone if I can help it—doing so is often not needed anyway.

I remember one time I was faced with gaining access to a private bank and had to make some hard choices.

Let me first explain the type of bank I was trying to infiltrate. You are probably familiar with the standard high-street bank, the type with bulletproof glass, CCTV, and, in some larger branches, security guards. All that security is really about deterring would-be assailants. I am assuming you have read the other chapters—most of this book deals with how I rob those types of banks. This bank was different, though.

Imagine you are wealthy. No, wealthier than that—we are talking beyond the wealth of an average A-list celebrity, the sort of wealth built on generations. You are the type of person who wouldn't be caught dead walking into a high-street bank. How would they deal with you? Like some pleb off the street? Don't they know who you are? You expect managed services: a person assigned to you who knows your name and your needs; the sort of management where you are in charge, and they do everything to help you. You don't normally deal in cash, but you might go into the bank to arrange payment for a new painting or transfer gold across the Atlantic.

These sorts of banks exist for these types of people. These banks look and behave very differently from normal day to day banks you might use. The bank I was challenged to get into, if I could, was a nondescript building in London with a large black door that had a gold roundel in the middle. A doorman with a bowler hat stood beside it like a hotel porter.

If you were not known to the doorman, you could show an ID card and eventually be let in. The bank did not have bulletproof glass inside, and there was little cash on hand—after all, it didn't have that type of clientele. The counters were solid oak, and the tops had brass finials that arched between small brass poles. Each teller's desk had one of those green lamps you see in movies, and the tellers were dressed impeccably, like concierges in a five-star hotel. There were green leather sofas, matching chairs, and marble busts on marble pillars representing past managers and clients who had donated to the bank. This bank looked the way we would all love our banks to look.

I figured I would never pass for one of the ultra-wealthy. It's not their clothes or assets; this type of individual has an air about them that exudes money, a far cry from the poverty I grew up in. I would have to impersonate someone to even get in the door, let alone into the back rooms. I had the perfect target in mind.

The Financial Conduct Authority (FCA) is a regulator that oversees banking in the UK. I wouldn't normally impersonate them, but doing so would get me through the door. I had no intention of using the ID card beyond that, and our legal team OK'd it, too, as long as I never actually said I was FCA. I created a fake ID card. Now the FCA does not have ID cards, so I made one up—that should have been the first warning sign that it wasn't real. I also made sure it didn't say FCA anywhere. It had my full name on it, though, and for design reasons, it had the letters FC hundreds of times in tiny writing as a background image.

I walked up to the doorman, and as predicted, he instantly assessed that I was not one of the bank's clients. He held out his hand to politely stop me and said it was a private building. I whipped out my ID card made of cheap plastic with an awkward photo stuck under the laminate and held it up without saying anything. I figured if I said anything, it might not help.

He snatched it and peered at me. He motioned for me to follow him in.

He indicated that I should sit on one of the chesterfield green leather seats next to a marble bust of a bald old man whose name was Arthur something the 3rd. There were two CCTVs in the entire building. The staff were shuffling papers like you see at the end of the news, busying themselves because there were no customers.

I waited silently and took in the surroundings. I figured either the police would turn up or I would be ejected.

What happened next was a bit of a blur. A small man in an ill-fitting suit and with a receding grey hairline appeared at a shuffling run, followed by the doorman, who went back to his post outside.

The small man turned out to be the branch manager, and he was overly nice. He asked my name but nothing else about me. Would I like tea? Biscuits? Don't mind if I do, thank you!

I was shown into a back room. The walnut-lined walls would normally have seemed oppressive and dark, but the expensive landscape paintings broke them up. He explained that he would be back shortly with "the others" and the tea and biscuits.

While alone, I took the opportunity to find a network access point in the room. Using a small remote access device, I was able to plug into the network. I could use this device later to remotely access their systems from the inside.

Shortly after that, the room filled with suits. I was introduced to multiple bigwigs, all of whom were keen to be nice.

We sat at the large oval table that dominated the room; water in crystal glasses was served, and the tea and biscuits appeared.

"So," said the small man. "What an unexpected visit. What can we do for the FCA?"

"Well," I said, "the thing is, I am not the FCA." Apparently they had mistaken the FC on my ID for FCC and from that point on assumed I was the FCA, because who else would be so bold as to come in and demand a meeting?

I wish I could convey the astonishment, the blustering, the huffs and puffs, and the downright outrage around the room over the next quarter of an hour as I explained who I was, why I was there, and how I got into this back room. I also explained the remote access device, unveiling it like a magician revealing an elephant to astonished gasps.

My card was passed around the table like a hot potato. Threats were made to call the police, but calmer heads prevailed, and my client was put on a conference call to clear up the confusion.

The trouble with places that use security by obscurity is that they become complacent. They assume no one will do anything out of sorts or go around their policies, procedures, or security controls. Like watching a child learn to ride a skateboard or bike, it is sometimes painful to watch a client learn these mistakes. But no matter how painful it is for them, I always make sure they understand that if a criminal had done the same thing, the consequences would have been more painful than they could imagine.

Chapter 61

How Maglocks Work

This is a somewhat technical chapter, and it's needed to help educate you about one of the most common security issues I come across daily: magnetic locks on the wrong side of doors.

What is a magnetic lock, or *maglock*? How does it work, and, more importantly, why the hell does it matter that we know?

Every security system has a flaw. The reason for the flaw is that it's how the system is meant to work. You could create a perfectly secure system, but it would be unusable. Physical security systems exist to allow only certain people in. So, to be effective, a security system must stop being a security system briefly and for the right reasons.

A maglock is a locking mechanism generally found on doors or gates. It consists of three components: a metal plate, normally attached to the top of the door; an electromagnet attached to the door frame; and a mechanism to authenticate against, often a badge reader by the door.

The mechanism for authentication can differ. How it works is not part of this chapter, but the end result is that if you are authenticated, the system cuts the power to the electromagnet.

Here is a little drawing I did to show how a maglock works.

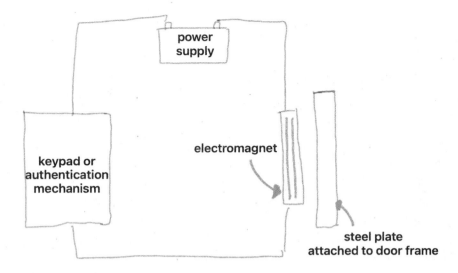

When it's locked, power runs to the electromagnet and prevents the metal plate from moving, keeping the door locked.

There are situations where you can force the two plates apart and gain entrance; some of the smaller locks will succumb to this brute force. Sometimes the door or the frame is weak and won't hold up to a person forcing the plates, thus allowing entry.

But another attack method works wonders on these types of locks. Unfortunately, criminals know this already; I will share it with you so that if you see this type of lock, you can point it out to the owner and get it fixed.

The system relies on power being sent to the electromagnet. If this power is interrupted, the lock can no longer function. Before you kill the power to the building or city block, be aware that many systems like this have a small battery backup that can often last a few hours.

However, if you have access to the wires that send the electricity to the electromagnet, you can safely cut those and unlock the system.

Some of you may have spotted the issue: how do you cut the wires without first opening the door? Well, this is the most common issue I see. If you look around your office or when visiting somewhere, you will see that the magnetic lock is installed on the outside of the door rather than the inside.

It looks a lot like this.

Every one of these locks has been installed on the outside—the side an attacker will approach from. Had these locks been installed correctly, you would not see the electromagnet or the metal plate it attaches to.

Keep an eye out for this super-common security issue.

Chapter 62

Personal Escort

People are helpful and nice, in general—look at the people around you, those you work with. I would confidently say that 80 to 90% of the people around you are nice, or maybe even more than that. The trouble is, nice and helpful folk can be a security nightmare if they are not trained in security issues and how people may take advantage of their kindness.

I once broke into an office for a client who tasked me with gaining access to particular rooms within the building. As always, there was a catch that made this harder than it should be. If it were easy, they wouldn't have hired me, right? And besides, it would make a boring anecdote for you.

The site had two buildings maybe 25 feet apart. Between the two buildings ran four corridors: two on the ground floor and two on the third (top) floor. These corridors were heavily secured. You had to go in via the lower-security side and pass the security systems in the corridor before you could access the secure building.

Pretty nice layout, and it worked somewhat well most of the time.

I made my way into the less-secure building and quickly found that I would be hard-pressed to get access through the corridor. I had to come up with another plan.

I located the executive area and came across a personal assistant (PA). They often have their own desk outside the executive area and are formidable forces of intelligence who are savvy to most attacks.

I was much younger than I am now and could easily pass as a newcomer to the company. So, I started to act nervous and unsure of myself as I approached the PA. She looked up as I fidgeted toward her. I managed to tell her that it was my first week, that I had no idea what I was doing, and that I had been sent up to arrange a meeting room. My boss had dumped this on me and left earlier in the day and would be back with a new client shortly. I was desperate to find the meeting rooms.

To be clear, I had done my recon: I had studied the employees and internal maps. I knew the meeting room I was after was about 40 feet from the room I needed to get into, and I knew the name of that meeting room. This is why recon phases are always the most important part of a test.

The PA was lovely, kind, and understanding about how intimidating everything must be. I grabbed my crumpled notes from my pocket and asked where the Heron room was.

"The Heron room? Sorry, that's not over here; it's over there in building 2." She broke the news to me while pointing to the corridor.

"Well, I am going to be fired, then. My badges haven't come through from security yet, so I only have this temporary one."

Again, for clarity, the temporary badge I had was homemade. I had observed a few people wearing them during my recon and made one that looked as close as I could. It certainly fooled the few who looked at it that day, including the PA.

I started to look panicked, and the helpful PA interjected. "I tell you what: as you have a temporary badge, I can walk you over."

"Wow, that would be amazing. Are you sure you can? Is that allowed?" I not only pulled on her heartstrings but also leaned heavily on psychology, which meant she had to prove she could do it.

And that is how a PA at this huge corporation escorted me through a couple of layers of security. We both had big grins on our faces, but for different reasons.

She showed me to the Heron room; she also showed me the system used for booking it and got my fake boss and me set up. We spent some time sorting out the monitor and phones, but it wasn't long before she had to get back to her own desk. As soon as she left me alone, I made my way to the intended target.

I want you to know that the PA never got into trouble for what she did; she was manipulated into actions that she would not normally have taken. I have left out some conversations for clarity and brevity, but social engineering is about this type of subtle manipulation. Had the PA not been so cooperative or not been around, I had a couple of other backup methods that I could have used to gain access to the other building. One was getting onto the roof, an entrance path I later pointed out to the client and that was also fixed. As a result of my assessment, the client also stopped handing out temporary passes.

In my career, I have had people hold doors open, help me remove items of value, and escort me to places of interest. This one stays in my mind because I can't believe it worked so well; having all the recon information in my head meant I could make up a situation that was believable and actionable on the fly. Recon really is the most powerful tool for an attacker.

Chapter 63

My Favorite Door

I want to share with you my favorite door. I know it's weird to have a favorite door, but this is mine. It's not a fancy door—believe me, I have seen some amazing ones, even nuclear bunker doors—but this is a door I found on a site that shocked me to my core.

Most people who know me would assume that my favorite door would be one that is super-secure. But in fact, my favorite door is the most insecure one I have ever seen.

Here it is.

You may look at this door and think it's pretty secure. I mean, it looks like it, doesn't it? You can see that it's shut, and it has a lock; and if you look really close, you can see that it has an alarm, too.

This door demonstrates that engineers, builders, installers, and even "security experts" don't always look at things the same way I do, I look at how to break in.

Let me guide you through what is wrong with this door. I promise it will make you look at doors differently; you might even impress someone with your new knowledge.

First up, the big sin: it's made of glass. This will come as no surprise to most of you, but glass has two properties that make it useless for security. First, it's see-through. That's how glass works; you can see through it. This is handy to attackers for many reasons; I could have written a chapter about the crazy things people have done with glass over the years in the misguided idea that design should come over security. Second, glass breaks. And it does so very easily.

Most of you are not criminals and do not need to think like one. If you've read this book, you may have wrongly concluded that criminals are smart if they use all the techniques I describe. However, I am simulating an advanced criminal type. The more common criminal type is dumb and lazy. Dumb and lazy criminals go for the easy way into places—even the dumbest and laziest criminal can hold a rock or a hammer and easily smash some glass. It would be rare for a criminal to come to your home when you are out, pick the lock, disable the alarm, and not set off the PIR lights in the garden. They are more likely to smash the window, grab stuff, and run.

My point is, don't make things out of glass if you want to be protected. That's strike one for our door.

Strike two: the magnetic lock I spoke about in Chapter 61. I hope you can quickly see that it's mounted on the wrong side of this door. What does that mean? Well, a more advanced attacker than our rock-wielding Neanderthal can cut the power and render the lock useless.

Sin number three: the alarm system. Security is often seen as a blocker rather than an enabler. Security allows us to do more things safely. An often-used analogy is the brakes on a car. If your car had no brakes, you wouldn't dare go very fast in it, right? But with the proper safety and security, you can push harder and go faster. I don't think it's a perfect analogy, but it kinda works. One of the worst things I see in my job is that people put the day-to-day use of a system before security. There should be a balance, but it has to be appropriate. Back to the door alarm: if you look very carefully (sorry, this picture is more than 10 years old), you can see a small grey box near the top middle, allowing the employees to turn off the alarm. A little weird that it's on the outside of the door—I mean, maybe they didn't want the noise for five seconds like a normal alarm. But look even more closely (and remember, this box is on the outside of the door with the attacker): for convenience, the client has left the key in the box. It's right there—the key . . . to the alarm . . . so anyone can turn it off. What on earth possesses someone to do that?

And we are not done with this door. Despite it being made of glass and having a pointless magnetic lock and an alarm system anyone can disable with the key left in it, there is one more sin related to this door.

If you study the picture, you might work out that this is not an exterior door; it's an inside door. I was standing in a tiny foyer, and the door behind me had no security; it was a door anyone could open and walk into. The "security" door was inside. That's not the sin, though; this setup is used in countless places, but normally it's done better.

Because this door was an afterthought of some security team and was pieced together by individuals who didn't understand security, they missed another vital issue. The building had what's known as a dropped ceiling: a suspended set of white tiles as you've seen in schools, offices, etc. There is a large gap between the white removable tiles and the solid ceiling above to help reduce noise, retain heat, and allow wires and lights to be installed easily. The trouble here is that the top of the door is protected by nothing more than a few removable white tiles. Any fool could climb up and over the door without smashing the glass, turning off the alarm, or disabling the maglock.

I love this door so much because I love teaching people like you about security, and the best way to teach people is to show them. A door like this gives multiple opportunities to teach others. I hope this becomes your favorite door too, and that you can pass on some security advice to those around you.

Chapter 64
Microwave Fences

Fences can be tricky. There are many types and many ways to circumvent them.

Fencing is like old castle walls. Interestingly, I once broke into an old castle by jumping over a small protective fence across a dry moat and scaling a small section of wall—breaking into a castle is relatively easy as long as people are not shooting arrows at you while you do it.

The point is, fences are fallible, as are all security measures. It's only when they are aligned with other security measures that they become a working security solution. Security is often seen as a black-and-white thing: something is secure or not secure. But it's more nuanced than that. Security provides a means to slow an attacker. On a long-enough timeline, an attacker will succeed at getting in. Fencing is the same; slow an attacker long enough that they will be caught.

I mentioned that there are many types of fencing: different materials, different heights, and even different methods of making them effective. Most can be bypassed in obvious and easy ways. Look at any fence for more than a few minutes, and I am sure you can figure out a way to cut, scale, or otherwise circumvent it.

People can add tricks and other security measures to a fence to make it feel more secure. For example, tremble devices let you know if the fence is being moved—the trouble is, foxes and other animals can set them off, too. You can have fancy toppers like razor or barbed wire or even glass—again, easy to overcome if you know how. I have even seen lasers protecting the tops of some fences. I have come across fences with underground tunneling detection and munitions deployed between two large fences to create a DMZ (demilitarized zone) or buffer area to prevent ingress and make it easier to spot attackers.

One of the stupidest fence systems I was ever asked to attack was an invisible barrier system called a *microwave fence*. This simple system offers nothing for the defender except ego and a large invoice.

Let me explain how it works before I share how I bypassed it.

Two posts are placed in the ground: one is a microwave sender, and the other is a receiver. One post sends a continuous signal to the other; if the other does not receive the signal, something is blocking the two posts. In that case, an alarm is signaled.

Microwaves are very hard to imagine, so picture the same two posts with torches: one sends a light, and the other looks for the light. If something blocks the light, the alarm goes off. The system is essentially looking for a shadow.

The key is that it's not a narrow beam like a laser. So, how did I get around this system?

In this case, a large bush had been planted in front of the entrance, creating a permanent shadow on the microwave beam, a place in the beam that is continuously broken and so its presence is adjusted for. This meant there was a two-foot gap underneath the fence. All I had to do to circumvent this ridiculously expensive system was crawl on my hands and knees. As I have said numerous times in this book, how security is put into the environment can be its undoing.

Here is a picture of the building and the bush; you can clearly see some of the green fencing posts.

Chapter 65

Discarded Passes

With companies providing onboarding training to all new employees, it astounds me that none appear to give any training about badges or passes beyond how to use them. For those of you who have never worked in an office, most employees are given a badge that can be as simple as a logo of the company you work for; other badges have your name and photograph on them, and some have security features to prevent counterfeiting. An access control system is almost certainly embedded, such as a magnetic strip or RFID wireless system that can be swiped against a door to allow access.

Badges provide visual security as well as a physical security mechanism. However, absolutely everything can be forged. I have copied, forged, and made from scratch thousands of badge systems.

The amount of access that the right badge can give you is obvious—you have seen throughout this book how a stolen badge has gotten me access to places. What isn't always obvious is how powerful even the lowest-privileged badges can be. Any badge is better than no badge.

When I say that people are not taught how to use a badge, I mean they are not taught when and where they should and, more importantly, *should not* wear them. For those people who have not gotten good training, here are some tips:

- Always wear your ID badge around the office.
- Never wear your ID badge outside your site, even if it's for a minute to move between buildings.
- Never leave your badge somewhere you wouldn't leave something precious.
- Never lend your badge to anyone.

In bigger companies, I often see temporary or visitor badges. These are usually more generically marked and are given at the start of the day and returned at the end of the day.

I have two anecdotes to show how these can be abused. During the first, I was a visitor to a secure building. As I was being escorted to the office space I would be using that day, I commented to my client that I did not see anyone wearing ID badges.

"Oh, most people don't wear them in this building."

"That's odd; how on earth do they tell guests from people who work here?" I asked, already guessing at the answer.

"Ah, that's easy. Anyone not wearing a badge probably works here, and those with visitor badges are obviously visitors," he said, as if explaining it made it better.

I grabbed my badge and yanked at the lanyard, breaking it apart, and swiftly put my badge into my pocket.

"Well, there we go; I now work here. I guess I don't need an escort!"

I could see that the chap was flustered and had no idea how to react. He just laughed, and we kept walking. This shows you how badge systems that are not thought out, let alone enforced, can easily be defeated.

Another anecdote highlights a bad practice I see with visitor badges.

A well-known bank requested some help in their HQ building, and I went in to look at the physical security. During my recon phase, I noticed that the bank issued generic visitor badges, which were returned as the guest left the building. The trouble was, because this was such a large, busy headquarters, the reception/security desk had found a way to deflect the collection of the passes: they had placed a cardboard box at the end of the desk with a sign saying "Return badges here," assuming that people would drop their badges in the box. Surprisingly, everyone did.

If I had a visitor badge, I wouldn't have to give it back, but that wasn't the issue with the setup. I was able to enter the reception area, go over to the box on the desk, and, when no one was looking, grab a couple of discarded visitor badges and walk off!

A few minutes later, with my new visitor badge around my neck, I approached the entrance gate for visitors and was let in.

I also often see valid badges for visitors left on reception desks; a small distraction and a quick grab will gain me a working badge in moments. Here is a photo of one such setup where you can clearly see the badges ready for pickup alongside blank ones.

Chapter 66

Bypassing Speed Lanes

I f you have gone into an office building at any point in your life as a visitor or an employee, you have almost certainly been asked to walk through a glass sliding-door barrier. These come in multiple styles, but they are all based on a single mechanism: allow only authorized pedestrians through the barrier.

The mechanism can be independent of the barrier, but it is normally an RFID-based proximity card that you wave nearby. Once the authorization is verified, the glass doors open and allow you access.

Security is always a balance between allowing someone or something to do the job intended and not allowing others access. The point of security is to allow that to happen in the safest possible way. These glass barriers are hindered by so many safety concerns that they are barely security systems. It is possible to tailgate many of them—that is, walk in behind someone else. How often have you held the door open for someone you don't know or asked someone to hold the door open for you? In restricted-access areas such as lobbies to apartments or hotels, it's normalized behavior. You are just helping a fellow human. However, when taken advantage of, you could be letting in a criminal.

Tailgating your way past a security barrier can be an easy way into any site. You can take advantage of human psychology to help you do this.

People hate having their personal space invaded by someone else, and you can use that to your advantage. I have used this trick many, many times. It works for any system used to prevent the passage of more than one person: man-traps, barriers, gates, etc. In fact, the smaller and tighter the system, the better!

First, pick your target; it has to be someone who looks nervous or appears to have a milk-toast persona. Build up some speed as you barrel into them and the barrier just as they walk through, and pretend you expected them to be gone as you rushed in. This makes them feel both at fault and disgusted with you for invading their space. Follow this up with profuse apologies and some flustered arm movements. This normally dissuades and distracts them from asking questions or, worse, asking to see your badge.

The trick can be enhanced if it is raining outside: remove your jacket and run in soaking wet. This is a fantastic excuse for not seeing them. The more awkward you can make this encounter, the better your chance of success.

My favorite anecdote about this technique was a successful attempt I made on a single-person man-trap tube. It had been raining, so I got soaking wet outside in my shirt before picking a target. I chose an alpha male-looking man wearing a frankly ridiculous-looking puffy jacket. Just as he entered the tube, but before the door closed, I ran into him slightly too fast, and this rather mistimed speedy encounter landed us stuck in the small glass tube at the same time. It got awkward super-fast; he was certainly feeling my presence and was not happy about it.

The bulky gentleman in his oversized puffer jacket and I, soaked to the skin, were encased together like sardines as the door closed us in. I won't repeat his expletives here; all I really remember is the incredibly loud squeaking of our wet clothes against the glass tube as the door rotated around us. We burst out the other side like a can of exploding cookie dough. He was angry and ran off in case I was homosexual, according to his volley of defenses. I just calmly walked away to my target.

Some of these barriers have an anti-tailgating alarm system. This consists of a low-power laser beam that fires across the gap at leg height—you can see it if you look closely the next time you see such a barrier. The beam expects just one person to walk through the barrier. A simple and brilliant design that means you cannot tailgate, right? But the system only has one sensor, and it can only tell two states: "I am not sensing anything, so it must be air" or "I am sensing something, so it must be a person." It cannot tell how big that person is or if, maybe, they have a big briefcase with them.

The alarm can do some simple timing; for example, the laser wouldn't be broken for 30 seconds by a normal person using the system. However, with practice and a lot of confidence, you can still tailgate these systems if you get close enough to a victim who has legitimate access to the site. It is surprising how close you can get to someone without them noticing! Try it out on loved ones around the house; it's not as creepy as it sounds.

There are also other tricks you can employ to bypass these barriers. The first is simple: jump them. I have become adept at getting over barriers smoothly so as not to attract attention. It's often about the speed you approach rather than the method you use; slowing down or, worse, stopping before the jump will attract attention. The trick is to swing your legs up and over rather than move your upper body too much.

Another trick to bypassing these gates is to understand that they operate at the whim of health and safety, which means they cannot use too much force to close in case they injure someone. So, pushing or holding open a glass gate is incredibly easy. Just be aware that sometimes an alarm will sound if you do this. In my experience, though, no one cares, and half of the alarms don't work.

Chapter 67

The Case of the Angry Man

Picture this: an international trading bank contacts us and wants a social engineering test. We often turn these down because pure social engineering tests always work—we prefer more in-depth physical security assessments. Two types of clients generally request social engineering tests: those who actually want them and those who don't but are forced to have one. This case was a mix of the two.

The company directors wanted it, but the chief security officer (CSO) definitely did not. He was downright abusive in scoping meetings and calls and obviously felt that this test of the organization's security was a slight against him. I should have turned the job down, but as it was only one person against it, I felt we could help the company. During one of the initial face-to-face meetings, the CSO jabbed his finger at me and shouted, "If I ever see you in my building, I'll tackle you to the ****** ground. I don't give a **** about your letter of authority. I'll even call the police!" He was asked to leave the meeting, which I took as a good sign to carry on. After all, the board seemed to want this, and they were being pleasant enough.

When I found out later that he had been brought in at a high salary and spent over £1 million on security in his first six months, the CSO's attitude started to make sense. He felt he knew everything, and it was his way or nothing. This assessment was a personal affront to his knowledge and skills.

Several months later, I started the assessment. It began late in the morning; within four hours, not only had I gained access to the building, but I had also essentially ruined the security of this multi-story building. All areas were compromised—I had broken through all the security systems, and the company's security was a joke. I was able to enter and exit the building multiple times and access every single area, including some that were supposedly restricted.

Frankly, after four hours, I had begun to get a little bored. This sometimes happens when a job goes well and the client has paid for me to be there all day. I started to wonder about the CSO who had threatened me during our initial meetings. People like him are normally a blocker to security; they always know best. I also hate bullies, especially those in the workplace.

I decided that on behalf of the bank, I had to stand up to him the only way I could. After all, he was part of the client, so I couldn't be too mean to him. But I did get the feeling that the board would appreciate him being taken down a peg or two.

I went back up to the floor that included his work area. It was pretty easy to find his desk. He was standing up, yelling loudly at someone on the phone and intimidating those around him. I half-pretended to use a photocopier as his conversation concluded; then he stormed off, swearing at no one in particular.

I waited a beat and then headed to his desk, where I spoke to his unfortunate desk neighbour. I asked where he was, as I needed him. "On lunch. He won't be back for an hour or so," came the reply—could I hear a hint of relief? I asked if I could leave a note. I sat in the CSO's chair and wrote a note to him using his notepad and pen. I left the note on his keyboard and kept his pen. Then I got up and wandered off in no particular direction.

After performing a few other actions that day, I decided to wrap up the assessment and get on with my report. I would present a summary to the board in the morning.

I got onsite early and was shown to the boardroom; several members were already there. The CEO and other directors were on the edge of their seats, waiting to find out how well they had done—when suddenly the door to the room burst open like someone had kicked it in. The CSO appeared and began shouting.

"Is that little ***** here yet? I am going to—oh, there you *********
are, you ******!" Having spotted me mid-opener, he stormed around
the table. He loomed over my seat, trying his best to intimidate me.
"What the **** is the meaning of this?" He threw a crumpled note
into my lap.

Keeping my composure as much as possible, I picked up the
note and flattened it out. I confirmed that it was the note I wrote
and passed it to the CEO very calmly before saying, "What it means
is, you are not doing a very good job."

The CEO stifled their laughter as they read my note and passed
it around the top end of the table. Each reader chuckled to themselves. Sensing that the tone in the room was now against him, the
CSO knew he had lost his battle. He stormed out the door with a
flurry of expletives.

The board members at the far end of the table were in shock,
and one said to the CEO, "What does it say? The note, I mean."

The CEO, now fighting back genuine tears of laughter, managed
to read the note aloud.

"Better luck next time, HA HA HA. I sat at your desk! And it's
signed by FC." They didn't even mention that I had put a smiley
face on it.

While that seems like a childish prank, it had real-world impli-
cations for the company's security. The CSO's attitude toward security and staff was working against what was best for the company.
My prank highlighted to the board that an abrasive counter-security
culture had taken hold. Those in security must realize that they do
not know everything. They should have a healthy paranoia, be open
to new suggestions, and, above all, be willing to work with people
who want to help them improve security.

Chapter 68
Let's Play Doctors

Almost everyone wanted to be a doctor when they were a kid. (Or maybe you wanted to be a firefighter or an astronaut.) Very few people pursue this dream when faced with the truly monumental tasks it entails.

To be honest, I never wanted to be a doctor or a fireman. Nor an astronaut, now that I think about it. But with hard work and dedication to my job, I can fulfill other people's dreams.

My passion has been and will remain computers and security, but that's not to say I haven't had the chance to play other roles more than a few times.

As you know, when I am not legally hacking into companies' computers to help improve their cybersecurity, part of my work is infiltrating buildings and helping clients with physical security. Often the two areas of digital and physical security cross over into a more holistic approach to security. It is often possible to gain access physically to a restricted space and then implant or infiltrate computer systems to either extract classified materials or perform some other action the client is worried about attackers carrying out.

Most of our clients are normal, everyday companies—some of you may even work for a company in this book. Our clients come from all sectors and industries. Hospitals, however, are rarely tested. The main reason is that they generally do not have the budget. We were happy to help the UK's NHS system with some of its cybersecurity during the COVID crisis as a piece of pro bono work, but in general, hospitals are not typical clients.

But private hospitals or those that have a large public view do come to us. Several years ago, we were contracted by such a hospital and asked if we could help with several areas of security, one of which was a mix of physical and cyber-related security testing.

Hospitals are weird places from a security perspective because they are essentially public buildings—anyone and everyone can walk into the building at almost any time of the day or night and any day of the year. The general public can be found in almost every department: those receiving care, those visiting those in care, those waiting for care, and those lost in the chaos of the building and trying to find where their elusive appointment is being held. When I was in my late teens, I remember wandering around a hospital in the early hours of the morning, trying to find an X-ray department when I broke my wrist. It was utterly deserted, with most of the lights off. I was hopelessly lost.

Hospitals are also mazes of corridors, multiple buildings, and many rooms. They are often a mix of very old buildings (sometimes hundreds of years) and modern glass and steel structures. And hospitals are among the most stressful non-war areas; no one goes to a hospital unless they need to be there.

In addition to the public areas, you have restricted areas. These are slightly more guarded, but the public can still be found there. These include surgery rooms, maternity and childcare areas, wards that hold patients on life support, and wards that hold biologically dangerous patients. All of these are semi-restricted.

The final areas are the few refuges for doctors, nurses, and administrative staff: offices, canteens, changing rooms, meeting rooms, etc. Depending on the size of the hospital, these areas may also include laboratories, record stores, and medical supply storage.

As you saw in Chapter 16, when I tried to steal a hospital helicopter, areas for medical vehicles are also highly controlled.

In this case, our job was to find and infiltrate those restricted areas. The hospital wanted us to perform a series of actions to provide proof but also to help highlight any security concerns the facility might have.

My wife and I decided we could blend in more easily as a couple than if I went in by myself—doctors and staff are less likely to confront a confused, fraught couple than a lone man.

Getting a layout of the hospital was incredibly easy. As I mentioned in Chapter 19, maps of the building were everywhere. It was built hundreds of years ago and expanded many times since, which meant, like almost all hospitals in the UK, it had extensive tunnels and underground areas. We entered the front of the building, breezed past reception, and headed toward the restricted areas.

Now, I want to assure you that we agreed there was zero sense or reason to enter any of the semi-restricted areas I mentioned or test the public areas. We did not want to interfere with patients or endanger anyone's care. For example, we would not go near the maternity ward or operating rooms.

While the maps helped us, the maze-like structure meant even we got a bit lost. The biggest issue was that some elevators serviced only certain floors, so getting to the right underground area was difficult. We wandered around the poorly lit tunnels, and besides having odd interactions with lovely people working there, we found all sorts of interesting things. We located the postal room where packages and mail were sorted. We even took a few security radios that we found charging unattended, to listen to in case security was alerted.

We figured we would go back there. But to carry on with our tasks, we needed a few extra items to help us blend in, so we went hunting.

Across the street from the main hospital was the main administrative building, an imposing brick structure with a single entrance. Inside was a tiny reception area with a security guard. Beyond that, we knew, were the IT department, executives, and other functions.

Our luck was overflowing that day: the front door was propped open for builders going in and out, so we could glance inside as we walked back and forth past the building. Suddenly we saw an opportunity and took it. We walked in just as a builder was walking out carrying some large items. Making sure we kept the builders and their items between us and the single security guard behind the reception desk, we sneaked into the main area. It took less than 3 seconds, and it worked a treat!

As we entered the main area, there was a short, wide corridor. To the left were restrooms, and to the right was a frosted glass room with several people inside (the type of room used by boards for big meetings).

We tailgated our way past the next internal door security system. We then came to a row of empty offices marked with names and titles. Obviously, our luck had held, and everyone from this area was in the meeting we passed on the way in. While my wife kept watch, I ducked into each office. On one desk was an ID badge. Someone this senior would have great access, so I removed it—and in yet another stroke of luck, the person's photo could, at a distance, be mistaken for my wife! She placed the badge around her neck, becoming an official staff member.

From this point on, gaining access was a breeze. The new pass opened 90% of the doors we needed—it was massively over-privileged in its access. By that, I mean an executive with the position she had did not require the access she had been given. On our journey around the restricted areas, we found the hospital's laboratories, each packed with expensive equipment. We found patient records where they shouldn't have been (and diligently secured them). But one of the most helpful things we found was an unlocked cupboard of fresh scrubs. We quickly locked ourselves into a nearby restroom and changed.

I had gone from security geek to full-blown doctor in minutes!

The irony is that my wife is an actual PhD doctor, but of engineering, not the type we were impersonating. It was my first time being a doctor, and I promise you we did not abuse the power that the badge and scrubs gave us.

The final part of this day highlights why we were originally brought in to help. The day-to-day staff's awareness of security was considered rather low, and the only task on our list that we had not so far achieved was to find the onsite server room for the main hospital computer systems.

We wandered around the tunnels for another half an hour but could not locate the server room. When we stumbled back into the post room we had found earlier, we decided enough was enough and asked one of the staff, "Where is the server room?" No explanation, just a straight question in an authoritative manner. It confounds me that asking for things often works.

The poor chap was confused. He didn't know what it was; he had never heard of it. He wanted to help us and looked crestfallen, while I did my best to appear slightly annoyed. But once I started to describe the server room, his eyes lit up. He could help me after all! He didn't know if it was the place we needed, as he wasn't allowed in, but it sure sounded like a room he knew of. He was so keen to help that he decided to escort us all the way there, eager to please someone he thought was important. He took us to a lift and got us through all the security doors using his badge. Finally, we stopped outside the double doors that secured the server room. We thanked him for his help, and he went back to the post room, leaving us alone to gain access to the most sacred area of the hospital.

Chapter 69

That's for Me!

It had been a long month. I had been traveling the country robbing banks for a client, and this was the last bank of 18. As you know from Chapter 50, I was given 18 banks to rob in one month, more than 5 per week, and I had been asked after the first week to change the strategy for every bank because I had been too successful.

The robberies continued to be a success despite being much harder.

When we plan these activities, the branch is not told any details; the fewer people who know, the better. This ensures a normal response and prevents leakage of vulnerabilities discovered and the chance of someone trying to game the results. What I mean is that if someone has any pre-knowledge of me or the attempt I am going to make (such as the date or the method), it can lead to false results and make the entire exercise null and void. To be honest, that is a huge waste of money for the client.

Even knowing as little as the fact that they are going to be tested soon can massively shift the way people behave (at least for a short time). If someone told you that a specialist was coming into your workplace in the next week or so to test how secure your facility is, I can guarantee you would change habits, start paying more attention to who is around you, and maybe even become a little paranoid.

The circle of trust on these types of jobs is therefore kept as small as possible, usually between three and five people. Small enough to know the details, and high enough to grant authority and corroborate and give assistance 24/7 if something goes wrong on the day. Because this assessment involved banks, we had to bring in another person for each job: the person overseeing the branch. Their role is to control multiple banks across an area, and they often are not in a single bank at all times but roam between branches to ensure smooth operations. As there was a risk of staff overreacting to what was going on and concern that the heads of such a large bank might not be contacted by branch staff, it was decided that bringing in the manager would provide a local source of confirmation and someone to help staff with a trusted individual. So, for each branch, we spoke to the manager and told them the rough idea and approximate dates. This way, they could be prepared. But they were sworn to secrecy for the reasons I already mentioned.

This set of high-street banks spanned the entire UK: 18 banks in total, each far from the next. I started up north and worked my way south and then back up into London. The London branches were spread across the city, but unlike the others, they were not as distant from each other. In fact, this became the start of the problem.

Two branches in the east of London fell under the purview of a single manager. No other branches crossed over like this.

As I have mentioned throughout this book, sometimes people react badly to the idea that a dedicated specialist is going to come and test them. Ego gets in the way of the bigger picture: they feel that the test is against them personally (or their work), and they hide that by deflecting it away from themselves. They say things like "You're testing my staff unfairly; they are not trained," or "You will ruin the trust the staff have." Both are true to a point, but that *is* the point. We are here to help staff improve and develop a mindset that is concerned about attackers.

Now and then a person reacts with verbal abuse or threatens physical abuse toward me. These cases are rare, and you can read about a few in this book. This branch manager reacted nothing like that. When I think back on that meeting, I feel that he was a little too silent. Unlike the other branch managers, he was quick to get the details and finish the call, but nothing weird raised a red flag.

A few weeks later, I entered his first bank, and although I was successful, it felt a little "off." When you do a job for a long time, no matter what it is, you get a "gut feeling." Little things were off for me, and looking at photos I took or recalling how the job went down should have made my gut feel a little more suspicious.

I can't go into details, but here is an example. Imagine walking into an office in the middle of the work day; everyone everywhere is busy, and every desk in the office is completely empty of anything except the bare essentials. People are clutching paperwork like it's their life insurance. People are doing everything they should be doing: double-checking that no one is tailgating them, locking computers, etc. It all felt a little unlikely. Despite all this, I was able to do what I needed to do. We had a washup meeting with the branch staff, and the branch manager was informed.

It's important to note here that I didn't get to talk to him personally. That should have been my warning that things were about to go sideways.

The next morning, I walked into the last branch on my list. I remember that morning pretty well, mostly because it's unusual for the UK sky to be nice and sunny, and I had breakfast outside at a small cafe opposite the bank. I sat in the sun eating a full English breakfast. (I live by the fact that you should always eat or sleep when you can.)

Around 11 a.m., just before the lunch rush, I walked into the bank and was greeted by one of those "roaming welcome" staff members. I gave her my story for the day, but I could see a slight nervousness in her eyes. I was politely directed to take a seat in the waiting area, and she rushed off to find the person I needed to see.

I sat next to an elderly gentleman with a folder of paperwork. He was keen to chat with me, and he explained how he was being screwed over by the bank. His mortgage rates had gone up, and he had family issues and health issues; how was he going to pay? He was on his third round of things that the bank couldn't have known about when I noticed I had been sitting waiting for way too long; there were also fewer bank staff visible.

I noticed furtive glances at me from the two who had remained. I also saw that some of the other customers who had walked in were helped immediately, and others were not taken to the reception area where I was seated but instead asked to wait in side rooms. I could tell what was about to happen, and here was this chap beside me, thinking he was having a bad day.

Just as the gentleman was telling me about the pain he had in his leg and how hard it was for him to get to the bank because of buses not running near his street, it happened.

Police cars with blue lights flashing and sirens blaring hurtled through the pedestrian area, and members of the public walking the street market scattered out of the way. The cars came to a halt near the bank, and several armed police response personnel rushed in. The fraught girl who welcomed me in extended her hands and pointed to the reception area.

With a deep sigh, I turned to the gentleman; he was having a sudden case of the shut-ups and had turned white with fright at the sight of the burly, military-looking men with guns. I leaned toward him, patted his knee, and told him, "Don't worry, that's for me!"

I never got to talk to the old man again, and I often wonder what he thought that day. I hope he got his mortgage issue sorted out.

You probably want to know what happened to me and why I still count this as a failure of the bank and not my work. Let me explain what went on during the 20 minutes I was waiting.

After my success at the previous bank, the branch manager was informed and apparently went ballistic at the staff; they had failed (not him)! He demanded every detail from them, asking to see the CCTV footage of the day and specifically of me. He then informed every one of his branches of those details and even handed out photos of me. By doing this and informing his staff, he ruined everything. From then on, the test was pointless because he had informed staff of likely days I was coming, what I looked like, the story I would probably use, etc. On top of that, they were told to forget de-escalation stages and other protocols for this type of situation and to call him personally as soon as they saw me.

Once I had been seated in the reception area, the overbearing manager was called: he told the staff to quietly remove as many clients as possible and to call the police and inform them of the robbery. He failed to mention to them that it was a *fake* robbery, that I was a good guy, and that I was there with permission from his bosses and bank owners. The staff, regardless of all they had been told, felt this was a real threat. I feel sorry about the stress he put on them that day.

Everyone was clear of the armed response area except the old guy who was unknowingly being used to keep me preoccupied. The manager had told the staff to leave him there as a distraction. Had this been a real robbery, he could potentially have been at risk, and I will never forgive the branch manager for that.

The response was swift; however, as it was a false call, it went against the branch and was noted by the police. False alarms are recorded by police, and too many may harm their response, even if the caller is a bank. Fortunately, I was able to talk down the police with the help of my emergency letter of authority.

This is where it gets interesting. I handed the real letter to the police (don't ever mess with them) but gave a fake letter to the staff. So, the police were able to talk to the client and verify everything. The staff skim-read the fake letter and ended up calling my friend, who, as per the script, told them everything was legit.

I left the bank that day having flabbergasted another small police unit that what I do for a living is a real job. It was late at night when I got home and was able to do hours of debrief with my client, which is how I found out what went down.

There was an obvious failure of the branch manager (he directed all the things that went wrong). But there were also policies and procedures for all staff to follow to keep the staff and public safe at all times. However, because of the branch manager's directions and the staff not feeling empowered to say no and to follow those procedures, all of those important steps were skipped. The situation essentially escalated to top-tier straight away. For example, I had made no direct threat, but they felt unsure of me, so policy stated that I should have been asked to leave. For example, they could have told me that the person I needed was unavailable or used some other excuse.

Not only did the manager fail, but the staff also failed to adhere to policy and procedures set by the bank. Another thing to note is that the staff were fooled by the fake letter and did not do as it stated ("use internal phonebook") but instead dialed the numbers I had given them. Never trust data that someone else provides you.

I later found out through a friend of a friend that the branch manager was let go because of his "toxic nature and reluctance to change his security outlook." He apparently sued the bank for wrongful dismissal, citing my assessment, which he said was an obvious targeted attack against him personally by bank board members who "hated him."

I often get to know that sites I assess get better because of my work; but this time I know that things got better for all the branches, not just because of my work but because of the bank's response to the manager's reaction. It definitely ensured that staff followed policies and procedures.

Chapter 70

How to Use a Snickers Bar

This title sounds stupid, doesn't it? Yes, you *could* eat the Snickers bar (that's one way to use it, and I love to do that), but I am talking about how to use a Snickers bar to break into a building. That's more like it! So, freeze it and throw it through a window? That is kind of cool, but it's not what I am trying to say here.

Let's back up a bit. I am talking, of course, about breaking into a building using other means, and the Snickers bar is just a way to help. When you are trying to get into a building, one of the easiest methods is to get someone else to help you. If a door is controlled by a security mechanism such as a PIN code or swipe-badge system, and you do not have access, you must get someone who does have access to let you in.

Seems simple, but how do you do that? You can't wait until someone comes up, puts in their code, and says, "You want to come in?" Well, sometimes you can, but most of the time, that won't work. You have to be sneaky!

You can sometimes tailgate: walk behind a person as they approach the door and go through and, if you have closed the gap enough, snatch the door handle before it closes and relocks. This technique can be effective but has its downsides. The biggest issue is when the person going through the door suspects you or glances back and sees you. Sometimes they are nice and hold the door open for you and then, heaven forbid, talk to you! You need an excuse to not be using your badge and not be able to talk to anyone who might question you.

Here is how to approach a door like this and prevent anyone from wondering why you didn't swipe your badge and from

231

verbally engaging with you. When another person is opening the door, approach with two items: a cup of coffee or a canned drink in one hand and an opened Snickers bar (or the equivalent) in the other. As you get near, make some noise to gain their attention.

When they look back at you, make gestures with your hands and slightly jog forward as you would when someone is holding any door open. These actions signal to the person that you are legitimate and expect them to hold the door open. They can see that you have both hands full and will not expect you to use the security mechanism. Now you have to prevent them from talking to you. This can be achieved by making eye contact with them and simultaneously placing the Snickers bar in your mouth. This leaves you with your mouth full, one hand holding coffee, and a free hand to grab the door. You can make appropriate eyebrow movements and nod as you grab the handle appreciatively and fumble around a little getting through the door. 99% of the time, this charade will make the other person not want to talk to you, let alone interrogate you about why you are not using the security system.

Variations of this technique can be used to your advantage: being a bumbling idiot, awkward, creepy, etc., can be a disadvantage in real life but can work in your favor when trying to break into a building!

Chapter 71

Taking the Bus to Work

Many people take the bus to work, cycle, walk, or take the train. I normally work from home, or I drive. But I doubt many people use transport the same way I do. I tend to use transport to circumvent security.

It was some years ago, but many of my jobs create a vivid memory that I can recall easily. I was tasked by a large tech company to perform a series of assessments against one of its more secure sites. The site was huge, housing multiple buildings within its perimeter. The entire place was very well protected; it had everything I often recommend to a client with a large budget.

Like many of the anecdotes in this book, I obviously can't go into many details (in this case in particular, someone who works there or nearby might be able to figure out where it is). But the perimeter was well-fenced and protected with multiple security features. The side and emergency exits through the perimeter were also well-secured. Even the main entrance gate was well-secured. Again, I wish I could mention some of the more interesting features of this site, but I do have to keep some things a secret.

Unlike most places with CCTV cameras, the multiple cameras here were watched by real security 24/7. The cameras looked over a barrier system that was physically manned at all times by guards. Anyone without a valid meeting was not allowed on the site. I even watched a few people who had legitimate reasons to visit be turned away. The few hundred people who worked there were not allowed to drive onto the site. Bikes were allowed, but security thoroughly checked anyone who turned up on foot or a bike.

There was only one way past this impressive security: to use their security against them. This happens more often than you would

233

think. Security is often installed as a barrier to entry—but it is almost always put in incorrectly or in a way that doesn't account for the ecosystem around it, which often opens more holes than if it wasn't there in the first place. Security becomes a crutch for those who do not understand it. A piece of technology added by non-security-minded people, often sold by a snake-oil salesman as the panacea to their problems, often ends up being a big, expensive mistake.

As the genius rapper Biggie Smalls once said, "Mo money, mo problems!"

I mentioned earlier that the employees were not allowed to park onsite. And this was the company's downfall. Because how do you get hundreds of people who drive to work into a site that doesn't allow cars?

Instead of onsite parking, the company had opted for a park-and-ride bus system for employees. "Bus" is maybe pushing it a bit far; it was a large van converted to have a bunch of seats in the back. The vans had no markings showing who they belonged to, but that didn't mean they were not obvious to someone taking careful notes. It also didn't take long for me to locate the other stop those mini-buses made. An unmarked parking area on the outskirts of town served as the bus-stop pickup area. It wasn't anything fancy, just a deserted piece of land with no barrier and a lone guard in a small wooden shack to keep an eye on things.

I drove into the parking area early one morning—very early, well before the main crowd of arrivals. I wasn't shocked that the old man sitting in his wooden shed did nothing—no check of who I was or if I was allowed to park there. I am not sure what would have gotten him out of that shack, but it certainly wasn't going to happen that day.

Typical of England, it was lightly raining. We have many types of rain in England; this was a fine "sticky" rain. It soaks you without being a downpour; it's one of the worst types. Because of the rain, I waited in my car as it steamed up inside. Finally, I saw one of the minibuses pull in. The first of the day!

I got out of the car and walked over to the minibus. The driver jumped out, ran to the left side, and opened the door, ready for passengers. He then went back to the driver's seat in the warmth.

I climbed into the minibus and sat down. He didn't even acknowledge me, let alone ask to see an ID badge. I mean, who can blame him? Who would be waiting in an unmarked parking lot at the crack of dawn and climb into an unmarked van if they didn't work for the company?

After a few minutes, a couple of other people joined me on the minibus. The driver did his little run in the rain, closed us in, and started the five-minute drive to the site.

So far, nothing groundbreaking in terms of security. I mean, so far, there had been zero security. But as we got closer to the site, my cunning plan to use the site's security system against itself would either work flawlessly or fail catastrophically.

As the van approached the barrier, the guard stepped to one side. He knew the company vans; he saw them countless times each day. The last piece of defense was an ANPR system on the gate. ANPR stands for automated numberplate recognition system: it is a computer-controlled camera system that reads the registration plates of vehicles. They are used in many places now, and you have probably come across them in parking lots where you live.

This system was used to automate the entry barrier by identifying vehicles on the allowed list: the CEO's car, other directors' cars, etc. Those vehicles were not checked by security—and that list included the minibus!

As the van came to a halt, the ANPR system did its thing, instantly recognizing the van as allowed. The barrier rose and cleared the entranceway. The van, with its tiny cadre of passengers, was whisked in. Not a single ID was checked—the security guards didn't look in or check badges. They assumed everyone on board was an employee. The driver walked off and let us debark on our own at drop off point. I decided to take a photograph before I got off and went to work.

That is how you use a minibus to break into a secure facility.